Meditations Before Mass

Other books by Romano Guardini
from Sophia Institute Press:

The Art of Praying

The Rosary of Our Lady

Learning the Virtues That Lead You to God

Romano Guardini

Meditations Before Mass

SOPHIA INSTITUTE PRESS
Manchester, New Hampshire

Meditations Before Mass was first published in Germany in 1939 as *Besin-nung vor der Feier der Heiligen Messe* by Matthias Grünewald Verlag, Mainz. An English translation entitled *Meditations Before Mass* was published in 1956 by Newman Press. In 1993 Sophia Institute Press published a slightly revised and edited edition under that same name. In 1997 Sophia Institute Press changed only the title of its 1993 edition to *Preparing Yourself for Mass*. This 2013 edition is an abridgment of the 1993/1997 edition with a return to the title *Meditations Before Mass* and includes a new introduc-tion. It is published with the permission of Matthias Grünewald Verlag, Mainz.

All quotations from the New Testament are taken from the Confraternity of Christian Doctrine edition, 1947; quotations from the Old Testament are from the Douay-Rheims version. The Psalms have been cross-refer-enced with the enumeration in the Revised Standard Version.

Sophia Institute Press
Box 5284, Manchester, NH 03108
1-800-888-9344

www.SophiaInstitute.com

Sophia Institute Press® is a registered trademark of Sophia Institute.

Library of Congress Cataloging-in-Publication Data
Guardini, Romano, 1885-1968.
   [Besinnung vor der Feier der Heiligen Messe. English]
   Meditations before mass / Romano Guardini. — Abridged edition.
     pages cm
   ISBN 978-1-62282-166-2 (leatherette : alk. paper) 1.
Mass — Meditations. I. Title.
   BX2169.G8313 2013
   264'.02036 — dc23

                                                             2013016831

Contents

Introduction

"*Sursum corda!* Lift up your hearts!"

I remember as a child watching my grandmother in church, standing in front of a statue of St. Lucy, tears flowing down her cheeks, her face radiant, and her lips moving ever so softly. I was mesmerized, and it touched my heart to watch her. From her I learned the prayer of the heart. Even though I never knew what she said to St. Lucy and to God, I knew in my heart that she prayed heart to heart with the Lord.

Lifting up our hearts to God is the goal of the Christian life. The heart in the biblical and liturgical tradition represents the whole person—mind, body, and spirit. "The heart is the dwelling-place where I am, where I live." It is our "hidden center" and "place of encounter" with God (*Catechism of the Catholic Church* [CCC] 2563).

When we are invited to "lift up our hearts" at Mass, we are asked at that moment to lift up our whole self to the Father. Even though the entire life of a Christian should be a constant raising of the mind and the heart to the one and eternal God, the Mass is a more intense, more intentional "lifting up."

The invitation to lift up our hearts at the most important part of the Holy Sacrifice of the Mass is an invitation by Jesus through the voice of the priest to give our hearts to the Father, as He gave His life for us. We prepare to make our hearts and lives a total self-gift to the Father as Jesus made Himself a total gift to the Father "for us" on the Cross.

We are constantly bombarded by images and sounds that overstimulate our eyes and ears and draw our hearts away from God and toward sin. Through our sins, our hearts become blind and dull to the things of God. When we enter the Church, we cross a threshold "from the world wounded by sin to the world of the new Life" (CCC 1186).

Although there are many images and sounds present in the Liturgy, there is one "image" that dominates the church building and the Holy Sacrifice of the Mass. That image is the crucifix — the Cross of Christ. The Paschal Mystery — the Passion, death, Resurrection, and Ascension of the Son of God — stands at the center of Christian worship. In the Mass the people of God are oriented to the Cross. Christ's redemptive action on the Cross is made present at every Mass and gives meaning to all the events of our lives. From the Cross we receive the graces necessary to be disciples of Jesus in the world.

We are instructed in the path of discipleship by the Sacred Scriptures proclaimed in the Mass. This is the "sound" that echoes throughout the Liturgy and to which we should attune the ears of our hearts. The Church formally presents us with God's actions in history in the Scripture readings selected for each day's Liturgy. Moreover, the prayers of the Mass are steeped in the Word of God. The Scriptures reveal God's saving plan for humanity while the Sign of the Cross discloses how real His love is. The Word of God proclaimed makes known the Word of God made flesh in Jesus Christ.

By participating in the Liturgy, we receive the Word of God as did the two disciples on the road to Emmaus. On the day of the Resurrection, they heard the Scriptures explained to them by that mysterious Stranger. Their eyes were not opened until "he took the bread and blessed, and broke it, and gave it to them" (Luke 24:30). Only then did they recognize Him. This is the same movement that takes place in the Mass through the Liturgy of the Word and the Liturgy of the Eucharist (see CCC 1346-1347).

Through instruction in the Word of God and nourishment in the Eucharist, the Second Vatican Council desired that the faithful be led to "give thanks to God" through "offering the Immaculate Victim, not only through the hands of the priest but also together with him, they should learn to offer themselves" (*Sacrosanctum Concilium* 48). This is the ultimate aim of the Liturgy — to lift up our hearts so that they will be united to Christ's self-offering to the Father. On the Cross, Jesus lifted up His heart to the Father. In the Mass, we lift up our hearts to participate in Christ's sacrifice made present to us in an unbloody manner.

In this book by Msgr. Romano Guardini, you will be guided to lift up your heart more fruitfully to the Lord in the Holy Sacrifice of the Mass. These short meditations will lead you to the "full, conscious, and active participation" in the liturgy envisioned by the Second Vatican Council (*Sacrosanctum Concilium* 14).

This work is the fruit of a pastor's heart. Msgr. Guardini's love for the Liturgy is revealed in each meditation, and his desire is that we come to know the presence of Jesus and His love for us. In response to the need of his congregation to prepare more worthily for the Mass, he originally delivered these brief reflections before he celebrated Mass. His parishioners, wanting to discover how to encounter Christ more deeply, arrived early to listen to their devoted pastor teach.

Introduction

Msgr. Guardini is still able to guide us in our own preparation for Mass. Sophia Institute Press newly edited this volume to make the chapters particularly suited for individual meditative reading before the Liturgy. Although written almost a century ago, Msgr. Guardini's words remain fresh to us today because of the wisdom his insights offer regarding the timeless Mass.

As I read the book, I thought to myself that the same concerns we deal with today Msgr. Guardini dealt with in the 1930s. Our times are even more challenging with many new distractions that he never knew. We are grateful that the voice of this great teacher can continue to instruct congregations through these meditations.

I encourage you to read prayerfully these reflections so that you may participate more fruitfully in the Mass, the "source and summit of the whole Christian life" (*Lumen Gentium* 11). I pray that after you read this book, the next time you hear the words of the priest proclaimed, "*Sursum corda!* Lift up your hearts!" you may full-heartedly respond, "We lift them up to the Lord!"

Archbishop Samuel J. Aquila
Archbishop of Denver
August 24, 2013
Feast of St. Bartholomew, Apostle

Meditations Before Mass

1

Stillness

When Holy Mass is properly celebrated there are moments in which the voices of both priest and faithful become silent. The priest continues to officiate as the rubrics indicate, speaking very softly or refraining from vocal prayer; the congregation follows in watchful, prayerful participation. What do these intervals of quiet signify? What must we do with them? What does stillness really imply?

It implies above all that speech end and silence prevail, that no other sounds—of movements, of turning pages, of coughing and throat-clearing—be audible. There is no need to exaggerate. Men live, and living things move; a forced outward conformity is no better than restlessness. Nevertheless, stillness is still, and it comes only if seriously desired. If we value it, it brings us joy; if not, discomfort. People are often heard to say: "But I can't help coughing" or "I can't kneel quietly"; yet once stirred by a concert or lecture they forget all about coughing and fidgeting. That stillness proper to the most beautiful things in existence dominates, a quiet area of attentiveness in which the beautiful and truly important reign. We must earnestly desire stillness and be willing to give something for it; then it will be ours. Once we have experienced it, we will be astounded that we were able to live without it.

Moreover, stillness must not be superficial, as it is when there is neither speaking nor squirming; our thoughts, our feelings, our hearts must also find repose. Then genuine stillness permeates us, spreading ever deeper through the seemingly plumbless world within.

Once we try to achieve such profound stillness, we realize that it cannot be accomplished all at once. The mere desire for it is not enough; we must practice it. The minutes before Holy Mass are best; but in order to have them for genuine preparation we must arrive early. They are not a time for gazing or for daydreaming or for unnecessary thumbing of pages, but for inwardly collecting and calming ourselves. It would be still better to begin on our way to church. After all, we are going to a sacred celebration. Why not let the way there be an exercise in composure, a kind of overture to what is to come? I would even suggest that preparation for holy stillness really begins the day before. Liturgically, Saturday evening already belongs to the Sunday. If—for instance, after suitable reading—we were to collect ourselves for a brief period of composure, its effects the next day would be evident.

Thus far we have discussed stillness negatively: no speech, no sound. But it is much more than the absence of these, a mere gap, as it were, between words and sounds: stillness itself is something positive. Of course we must be able to appreciate it as such. There is sometimes a pause in the midst of a lecture or a service or some public function. Almost invariably someone promptly coughs or clears his throat. He is experiencing stillness as a breach in the unwinding road of speech and sound, which he attempts to fill with something, anything. For him the stillness was only a lacuna, a void that gave him a sense of disorder and discomfort. Actually, it is something rich and brimming.

Stillness is the tranquillity of the inner life, the quiet at the depths of its hidden stream. It is a collected, total presence, a being all there, receptive, alert, ready. There is nothing inert or oppressive about it.

Attentiveness—that is the clue to the stillness in question, the stillness before God.

What then is a church? It is, to be sure, a building having walls, pillars, space. But these express only part of the word *church*, its shell. When we say that Holy

Mass is celebrated "in church," we are including something more: the congregation. Congregation, not merely people. Churchgoers arriving, sitting, or kneeling in pews are not necessarily a congregation; they can be simply a roomful of more or less pious individuals. Congregation is formed only when those individuals are present not only corporally but also spiritually, when they have contacted one another in prayer and step together into the spiritual "space" around them; strictly speaking, when they have first widened and heightened that space by prayer. Then true congregation comes into being, which, along with the building that is its architectural expression, forms the vital church in which the sacred act is accomplished. All this takes place only in stillness; out of stillness grows the real sanctuary. It is important to understand this. Church buildings may be lost or destroyed; then everything depends on whether the faithful are capable of forming congregations that erect indestructible "churches" wherever they happen to find themselves, no matter how poor or dreary their quarters. We must learn and practice the art of constructing spiritual cathedrals.

We cannot take stillness too seriously. Not for nothing do these reflections on the Liturgy open with it. If someone were to ask me what the liturgical life begins with, I should answer: with learning stillness. Without it, everything remains superficial, vain. Our understanding of stillness is nothing strange or aesthetic. Were we to approach stillness on the level of aesthetics—of mere withdrawal into the ego—we should spoil everything. What we are striving for is something very grave, very important, and unfortunately sorely neglected: the prerequisite of the liturgical holy act.

2

Silence and the Word

We have discussed stillness in the presence of God. Only in such stillness, it was contended, can the congregation fundamental to the sacred ritual come into being. Only in stillness can the room in which Holy Mass is celebrated be exalted into a church. Hence the beginning of divine service is the creation of stillness. Stillness is intimately related to speech and the word.

The word is a thing of mystery, so volatile that it vanishes almost on the lip, yet so powerful that it decides fates and determines the meaning of existence. A frail structure shaped by fleeting sound, it yet contains the eternal: truth. Words come from within, rising as sounds fashioned by the organs of a man's body, as expressions of his heart and spirit. He utters them, yet he does not create them, for they already existed independently of him. One word is related to another; together they form the great unity of language, that empire of truth-forms in which a man lives.

Silence and the Word

The living word arranges itself onion-like in various layers. The outermost is that of simple communication: news or a command. These can be conveyed artificially, as they often are, by the printed word or by some sound-apparatus that reproduces human speech. The syllables thus produced draw their significance from genuine language, and they answer specific needs well enough. But this superficial, often mechanical, level of words is not yet true speech, which exists only in proportion to the amount of inner conviction carried over from the speaker to that which is spoken. The more clearly his meaning is embodied in intelligible sounds, and the more fully his heart is able to express itself, the more truly does his speech become living word.

The inmost spirit lives by truth, by its recognition of what is and what has value. Man expresses this truth in words. The more fully he recognizes it, the better his speech and the richer his words. But truth can be recognized only from silence. The constant talker will never, or at least rarely, grasp truth. Of course even he must experience some truths; otherwise he could not exist. He does notice certain facts, observe certain relations, draw conclusions and make plans. But he does not yet possess genuine truth, which comes into being only when the essence of an object, the significance of a relation, and what is valid and eternal in this world reveal themselves. This requires the spaciousness, freedom, and pure receptiveness of that inner "clean-swept room" which silence alone can create. The constant talker knows no such room within himself; hence he cannot know truth. Truth, and consequently the reality of speech, depends upon the speaker's ability to speak and to be silent in turn.

But what of fervor, which lives on emotion and emotion's evaluation of the costliness and significance of things? Doesn't fervor flow more abundantly into speech the more immediate the experience behind it? And doesn't that immediacy remain greatest the less one stops to think? That is true, at least for the moment. But it is also true that the person who talks constantly grows empty, and his emptiness is not only momentary. Feelings that are always promptly poured out in words are soon exhausted. The heart incapable of storing anything, of withdrawing into itself, cannot thrive. Like a field that must constantly produce, it is soon impoverished.

Only the word that emerges from silence is substantial and powerful. To be effective it must first find its way into open speech, although this is not necessary for some truths: those inexpressible depths of comprehension of one's self, of others, and of God. For these the experienced but unspoken suffices. For all others, however, the interior word must become exterior. Just as there exists a perverted variety of speech — talk — there exists also a perverted silence — dumbness. Dumbness is just as bad as garrulity. It occurs when silence, sealed in the dungeon of a heart that has no outlet, becomes cramped and oppressive. The word breaks open the stronghold. It carries light into the darkness and frees what has been held captive. Speech enables a man to account for himself and the world and to overcome both. It indicates his place among others and in history. It liberates. Silence and speech belong together. The one presupposes the other. Together they form a unit in which the vital man exists, and the discovery of that unit's namelessness is strangely beautiful. We do know this: man's essence is enclosed in the sphere of silence/speech just as the whole earthly life is enclosed in that of light/darkness, day/night.

Consequently, even for the sake of speech we must practice silence. To a large extent the Liturgy consists of words that we address to and receive from God. They must not degenerate into mere talk, which is the fate of all words, even the profoundest and holiest, when they are spoken improperly. In the words of the Liturgy, the truth of God and of redeemed man is meant to blaze. In them the heart of Christ — in whom the Father's love lives — and the hearts of His followers must find their full expression. Through the liturgical word our inwardness passes over into the realm of sacred openness which the congregation and its mystery create before God. Even God's holy mystery—which was entrusted by Christ to His followers when He said, "As often as you shall do these things, in memory of me shall you do them"—is renewed through the medium of human words. All this, then, must find room in the words of the Liturgy. They must be broad and calm and full of inner knowledge, which they are only when they spring from silence. The importance of silence for the sacred celebration cannot be overstressed—silence which prepares for it as well as that silence which establishes itself again and again during the ceremony. Silence opens the inner fount from which the word rises.

3

Silence and Hearing

Silence and speech are interdependent. Together they form a nameless unit that supports our spiritual life. There is, however, another element essential here: hearing.

Let us imagine for a moment a Dialogue Mass. Epistle and Gospel — indeed, a substantial part of the Mass is read aloud in English. What do those believers who love the Liturgy and wish to participate in it as fully as possible do? They take their missals in hand and read along with the reader. They mean well; they are eager not to miss a word; yet how odd the whole situation is! There stands the reader. Solemnly he reads the sacred words, and the believers he is addressing read with him! Can this be a genuine form of the spiritual act? Obviously not. Something has been destroyed.

Solemn reading requires listening, not simultaneous reading. Otherwise why read aloud at all? Our bookish upbringing is to blame for this unnaturalness. Most deplorably, it encourages people to read when they should listen. As a result, the fairy tale has died and poetry has lost its power; for its resonant, wise, fervent, and festive language is meant to be heard, not read. In Holy Mass, moreover, it is a question not only of beautiful and solemn words, but of the Divine Word.

This question is vital. In silent reading that frail and powerful reality called word is incomplete. It remains unfinished, entangled in print, corporal; vital parts are still lacking. The hurrying eye brings fleeting images to the imagination; the intelligence gains but a hazy "comprehension," and the result is of small worth. What has been lost belongs to the essence of the liturgical event. No longer does the sacred word unfold in its full spiritual-corporal reality and soar through space to the listener, to be heard and received into his life. Would it be a loss if men ceased to convey their most fervent thoughts in living speech and instead communicated with each other only in writing? Definitely. All the bodily vitality of the ringing word would vanish. In the realm of faith also the loss would be shattering. After all, Christ Himself spoke of hearing. He never said: "He who has eyes to read, let him read" (cf. Matt. 11:15). This is no attempt to devalue the written word, which in its place is good and necessary, but it must not crowd out what is better, more necessary, and beautiful: hearing, from which, as St. Paul tells us, springs faith (Rom. 10:17).

Faith can, of course, be kindled from the written text, but the Gospel—the glad tidings—gains its full power only when it is heard. The whole word is not the printed, but the spoken, in which alone truth stands free. Only words formed by the human voice have the delicacy and power that is necessary to stir the depths of emotion, the seat of the spirit, the full sensitiveness of the conscience. Like the sacraments, God's word is spiritual-corporal; like them, it is meant to nourish the spirit in flesh-and-blood man, to work in him as power. The saving God who came to us was the eternal Word. But that Word did not come in a blaze of spiritual illumination or as something suddenly appearing in a book. He "was made flesh" (John 1:14), flesh that could be seen, heard, grasped with hands, as St. John so graphically insists in the opening lines of his first letter. The same mystery continues in the living word of liturgical proclamation, and it is all important that the connection remain vital.

The word of God is meant to be heard, and hearing requires silence.

To be sure that the point is clear, let us put it this way: how may proper hearing be prevented? I could say something to a man sitting out of earshot, for example. Then I would have to speak louder in order to establish the physical connection. Or I could speak loudly enough, but if his attention is elsewhere, my remarks will go unheeded. Then I must appeal to him to listen. Perhaps he does listen, notes what I say, follows the line of thought, tries his best, yet fails to understand. Something in him remains closed. He hears my reasons, follows them intellectually and psychologically; he would understand at once if they applied to someone else. In regard to himself, he fails to see the connection because his pride will not admit the truth; perhaps a secret voice warns him that, were he to admit it, he would have to change things in his life that he is unwilling to change. The more examples we consider, the more clearly we realize that hearing, too, exists on many levels, and we begin to suspect its importance when the Speaker is God. Not for nothing did our Lord say: "He who has ears to hear, let him hear" (Matt. 11:15; Mark 4:9; Luke 8:8).

To have ears to hear requires grace, for God's word can be heard only by him whose ears God has opened. He does this when He pleases, and the prayer for truth is directed at that divine pleasure. But it also requires something that we ourselves desire and are capable of: being inwardly present; listening from the vital core of our being; unfolding ourselves to that which comes from beyond, to the sacred word. All this is possible only when we are inwardly still. In stillness alone can we really hear. When we come into church from the outside our ears are filled with the racket of the city, the words of those who have accompanied us, the laboring and quarreling of our own thoughts, the disquiet of our hearts' wishes and worries, hurts and joys. How are we possibly to hear what God is saying? That we listen at all is something; not everyone does. It is even better when we pay attention and make a real effort to understand what is being said. But all this is not yet that attentive stillness in which God's word can take root. This must be established before the service begins, if possible in the silence on the way to church, still better in a brief period of composure the evening before.

4

Composure

In the religious life silence is seldom discussed alone. Sooner or later its companion, composure, demands attention. What then do we mean by *composure*? As a rule, a man's attention is broken into a thousand fragments by the variety of things and persons about him. His mind is restless; his feelings seek objects that are constantly changing.

Composure works in the opposite direction, rescuing man's attention from the sundry objects holding it captive and restoring unity to his spirit. It frees his mind from its many tempting claims and focuses it on one, the all important. It calls the soul that is dispersed over myriad thoughts and desires, plans and intentions back to itself, reestablishing its depth.

All things seem to disquiet man. The phenomena of nature intrigue him; they attract and bind. But because they are natural they have a calming, collecting influence as well. It is much the same with those realities that make up human existence: encounter and destiny, work and pleasure, sickness and accident, life and death. All make their demands on man, crowding him in and overwhelming him; but they also give him earnestness and weight.

What is genuinely disastrous is the disorder and artificiality of present-day existence. We are constantly stormed by violent and chaotic impressions. At once powerful and superficial, they are soon exhausted, only to be replaced by others. They are immoderate and disconnected, one contradicting, disturbing, and obstructing another.

This state of affairs exists not only around us but within us. To a large extent man lives without depth, without a center, in superficiality and chance. No longer finding the essential within himself, he grabs at all sorts of stimulants and sensations; he enjoys them briefly, tires of them, recalls his own emptiness, and demands new distractions. He touches everything brought within easy reach of his mind by the constantly increasing means of transportation, information, education, and amusement; but he doesn't really absorb anything. He is happiest when in the thick of things, in the rush and noise and stimulus of quick results and successes. The moment quietness surrounds him, he is lost.

This state makes itself felt generally: in the religious life, in church services, in Holy Mass. Constant unrest is one of its earmarks. Then there is much gazing about, un-called-for kneeling and standing up, reaching for this and that, fingering of apparel, coughing, and throat-clearing. Even when behavior remains outwardly controlled, an inner restlessness is clearly evident in the way people sing, listen, respond—in their whole bearing. They are not really present; they do not vitally fill the room and hour: they are not composed.

Composure is more than freedom from scattered im-pressions and occupations. It is something positive; it is life in its full depth and power. Left to itself, life will al-ways turn outward toward the multiplicity of things and events, and this natural inclination must be counterbal-anced. Consider, for a moment, the nature of respiration. It has two directions: outward and inward. Both are vital; each is part of this elementary function of life; neither is all of it. A living organism that only exhaled or only inhaled would soon suffocate. Composure is the spiritual man's "inhalation," by which, from deep within, he col-lects his scattered self and returns to his center.

Only the composed person is really someone. Only he can be seriously addressed as one capable of replying. Only he is genuinely affected by what life brings him, for he alone is awake, aware. And he is not only wide awake in the superficial sense of being quick to see and grab his advantage—this is a watchfulness shared also by birds and ants. What we mean is true awareness: that inner knowledge of the essential; that ability to make responsible decisions; sensitivity, readiness, and joy.

Once composure has been established, the Liturgy is possible.

Not before. It is not much use to discuss Holy Scripture, the deep significance of symbols, and the vitality of the liturgical renewal if the prerequisite of earnestness is lacking. Without it, even the Liturgy deteriorates to something "interesting," a passing vogue. To participate in the Liturgy seriously we must be mentally composed. But, like silence, composure does not create itself; it must be willed and practiced.

Above all, we must get to church early in order to "tidy up" inwardly. We must have no illusions about our condition when we enter the church; we must frankly face our restlessness, confusion, disorder. To be exact, we do not yet really exist as persons—at least not as persons God can address, expecting a fitting response. We are bundles of feelings, fancies, thoughts, and plans all at cross-purposes with each other. The first thing to do, then, is to quiet and collect ourselves. We must be able to say honestly: "Now I am here. I have only one thing to do—participate with my whole being in the only thing that counts, the sacred celebration. I am entirely ready."

Once we attempt this, we realize how terribly distraught we are. Our thoughts drag us in all directions: to the people we deal with, family, friends, adversaries; to our work; to our worries; to public events; to private engagements. We must pull our thoughts back again and again and again, repeatedly calling ourselves to order. And when we see how difficult it is, we must not give up but realize only the more clearly that it is high time we returned to ourselves.

But is it possible at all? Isn't man hopelessly given over to outward impressions, to the press of his desires and his own unrest? The question brushes the ultimate: the difference between man and animal.

An animal is never truly distracted. In the exact sense we were using, it can be neither distracted nor composed; it has not yet been confronted with this either-or. Its own nature determines its existence and requires it to be in order. Only man can be distracted, because something in his spirit reaches beyond mere nature. The spirit can turn to the things of the world and lose itself there; the same spirit can also overcome distraction and fight its way through to composure.

Composure

There is something mysterious about the spirit, something relevant to eternity. Absolute rest and composure is eternity. Time is unrest and dispersion; eternity is rest and unity, not inactivity or boredom—only fools connect these with it. Eternity is the brimming fullness of life in the form of repose. Something of eternity is deep within us.

Let us call it by the beautiful name the spiritual masters use, the "ground of the soul" or the "peak of the spirit." In the first it appears as the repose of the intrinsic, of depth; in the second as the tranquillity of remoteness and the heights. This seed of eternity is within me, and I can count on its support. With its aid I can step out of the endless chase; I can dismiss everything that does not belong here in God's house; I can grow still and whole so that I can honestly reply to His summons: "Here I am, Lord."

5

Composure and Action

Just as proper speech and hearing emerge from silence, proper bearing and good action emerge only from composure. Action is more than mere external happening. It has innumerable levels, as many as life itself. There are purely external functions, such as turning on a light: if the switch clicks properly, the light burns without further ado. But if I am performing some real task, particularly something important, I must concentrate on it or there will be mistakes.

In the relations between people—service, friendship, love—in everything that belongs to the sphere of man and his work, work is genuine only in the degree that the doer inwardly participates in it. Colloquial speech has several telling expressions for this: he is "completely absorbed" in his work, or "his heart isn't in it." I can do a thing, alone and unaided, and still put very little of myself into it. My body goes through motions and some mental activity is exerted, but on the whole my mind is elsewhere—and the work proceeds accordingly. The nobler, the more difficult, or the more important the task to be accomplished, the more completely must I give it my attention, earnestness, eagerness, and love, participating in it from the heart and with all the creative élan of the mind. That is composure: heart and mind concentrated on the here and now, not off on daydreams; it is being all here.

This is true of all action, but particularly true of that which concerns us here, the service performed before God. The Liturgy is based on the fact of God's presence in the church. It demands as a response that we appear before that presence. But one must be really present—with body, mind, and soul, with attention, reverence, and love. That is composure. Only he who is composed can have God's presence within him and appear before Him to respond to His outpouring grace with adoration and love.

Composure also makes possible the proper outward bearing.

People's behavior in church is often so lax that even at the risk of sounding exaggerated, I must call attention to it. Many churchgoers simply do not seem to know where they are or what it is all about. A man's presence in church does not mean merely that his body is there rather than elsewhere. His body is the equivalent of himself, and being present is a vital act. *To be present*, then, is more than to sit or kneel in place. It is an act of the spirit and expresses itself in one's whole bearing.

Much the same is true of our various movements and gestures. Is there anything more embarrassing than the manner in which some people, upon entering a church, after an anemic genuflection immediately flop into their seats? As for sitting itself, in church it signifies more than mere comfort; it is the position of attentive listening. Similarly, kneeling here is quite different from the position a hunter might assume while taking aim; it is the offering of our erect position to God. And again, standing in church is a profounder act than that of a mere halt while walking, or the attitude of expectant waiting; it is the bearing of reverence before the heavenly Lord. We can do these things convincingly only when we are fully conscious of what is taking place around us, and that awareness is ours only when we are self-collected and composed.

Equally elementary and self-understood, yet equally in need of vigilance, are our acts of looking and seeing. Later we shall discuss in more detail the importance of the visual act in the divine service. It means more than the bird's discovery of a kernel or the deer's cautious survey of a landscape. It is the act by which a man grasps the essence of an object that he sees before him. To see something is the first step toward sharing in it.

Sometimes in the theater we come upon a face intent on the performance. The sight of another completely disarmed and self-forgotten can be so strong as to embarrass, and quickly we turn away. A man's eyes contain the whole man. To gaze full of faith at the altar means a great deal more than merely to look up in order to see how far the sacred ceremony has progressed.

Once in the cathedral of Monreale in Sicily I had the wonderful experience of watching the believers participate in the blessing of the fire and of the Paschal Candle on Easter Saturday. The ceremonies lasted over five hours and were not yet finished when I had to leave. The people had no books, and they did not recite the Rosary; they only gazed — but with all their souls.

How much of this visual power has been lost! There are many reasons for this: the vast amount of reading we do, the countless impressions of city life, news services, movies. Ultimately, they are largely to blame for the widespread loss of that composure which is still possessed by the simple man brought up in the Christian tradition. The gaze directed to the altar is exactly as profound as the composure from which it comes.

Or suppose we consider the gestures of the Liturgy; for instance, the simplest and holiest of all, the Sign of the Cross. Isn't the way it is often made an out-and-out scandal, no better than the careless, crippled greeting a man makes in passing to someone of indifferent interest? Certainly it is not the gesture with which we sign our bodies with the symbol of Christ's death and flood our souls with the vision of salvation, with which we acknowledge ourselves His and place ourselves under His power.

We do not come to church to attend the service as a spectator, but in order, along with the priest, to serve God. Everything we do—our entering, being present, our kneeling and sitting and standing, our reception of the sacred nourishment—should be divine service. This is so only when all we do overflows from the awareness of a collected heart and the mind's attentiveness.

Such composure is all the more necessary since liturgical action is devoid of that which otherwise enforces attention—namely, utility. When I seat myself at my desk and pick up a manuscript, my attention naturally passes to it; when I do a job in my workshop, I unconsciously pull myself together; otherwise it will miscarry. Everywhere some utilitarian purpose to be accomplished binds my attention. In the Mass there are no such purposes. The believer simply steps into the presence of his

God and remains there for Him. The Liturgy is a thing of exalted purposelessness, but it is filled with the sense of sacred serving, and over it reigns the sublimity of God. Here composure means everything. Hence it must be willed and practiced. Otherwise our "service" grows dull, indolent, careless, an insult to divine Majesty.

6

The Offertory

Until now our attention has been directed mainly to the liturgical word. But Holy Mass does not consist only — or even primarily — of words, although the Liturgy does include forms of divine service of which this is true: vespers, or choral prayer generally. The Mass, on the other hand, is fundamentally an act. The words the Lord used to establish it do not run: "Say this in memory of me" or "Consider, proclaim, praise what has taken place," but "Do." True, the Mass begins as an oral service and stretches as such from the preparation at the foot of the altar to the Credo, and it resumes this nature toward the end (from the Communion to the Last Gospel). Between the two parts comes action: the gift-offerings are prepared; the mystery of the Transubstantiation is executed; the sacred nourishment is proffered and received. Thus the believer's task consists not only in hearing and speaking the text of the Mass but also in taking part in the sacred act, and once again the prerequisite of participation is inner composure.

Today it is not easy to speak of genuine participation. This is due largely to the development that the Liturgy of the Lord's memorial has undergone. The first congregation was the group of disciples at table. This original form of community at table continued for a short time, as long as the congregations were very small. The Acts of the Apostles describe them: "And continuing daily with one accord in the temple, and breaking bread in their houses, they took their food with gladness and simplicity of heart, praising God and being in favor with all the people. And day by day the Lord added to their company such as were to be saved" (Acts 2:46-47). Here all still participate directly in the execution of the sacred act: they sit together at table over the divine Supper. We get the same picture from the first letter to the Corinthians (1 Cor. 10:15-17; 11:17-34).

Then, however, the congregations began to grow, and their numbers forced a new form on the sacred action. It lost its original, immediate character and became stylized, transposed to the plane of the liturgical-sacramental. In place of the realistic act we now have its symbolic representation. Table became altar and thereby lost something of its direct associations. A large number of people was less able to participate than a small number, and involuntarily the believer's attitude shifted to that of a mere observer. The whole became more and more sharply divided into two parts: here the altar on which the sacred act is ritually executed; there the people, aware that they are represented by the priest, but no longer actually seated at table. As time went on and the rooms for divine service became larger, the new form took over more consistently; today little remains of the original form — strictly speaking, only the collection after the Offertory and the Communion rail.

Certain details of the early form of the Mass could undoubtedly be restored. First of all, without innovations and artificialities, the Offertory could be developed so that its original sense is thrown into sharper relief and the congregation could participate in it more fully. In general, however, historical development cannot be turned back. As long as congregations have the size they must have at present, the possibility of direct participation will necessarily remain limited. It is up to us to see to it that participation does not consist only of these outward details.

To participate means to share in the task of another. Here that other is the priest. He is there not for himself but for the congregation. By means of the words he speaks and the gestures he makes in the power of his office, something happens—through Christ. Everyone present is called upon to share in that happening. The priest responds to it, not privately for himself but for all. And again all are invited to share in his invocation, celebration, adoration, pleading, and thanksgiving. The celebrant's actions radiate in all directions far beyond his personal life. This is so primarily that all may—and should—enter into them.

How does such entry take place? First of all, through the participants' vital awareness of what is happening. When the Offertory prayer is spoken and the priest uncovers the chalice, we should say to ourselves: "Now the gift-offerings with which the mystery will be celebrated are being prepared. What the Lord instructed His disciples to do when He told them to prepare for the feast of the Passover, and what the first congregations did when each believer stepped forward with his offering of bread, wine, and oil, is being done—now." Today all the preparations have been telescoped to the brief movements with which the priest lifts up the paten with the Host and replaces it, receives the wine from the server, pours and mixes it with water, raises the chalice, and puts it down again.

Here we must realize that these few gifts on the altar stand for all that was formerly given and done in preparation for the Lord's Supper and for the needs of the poor brothers and sisters in Christ; whatever is done for the least of these is done "for me." Something else belongs with the bread and wine: the money offering of the faithful, [which] represents the abundant, personal gifts once brought to the altar. A poor representative, to be sure! How much more alive this act was when one brought bread from his own oven, another a jug of wine, a third a jar of oil. Now we have only cold coin. But we should neither lament what is past nor dream of future impossibilities; money is the modern substitute for goods. Hence our participation in the offering demands that this impoverished gesture be made as well as possible. We must not, for example, start fishing for our gift in church, breaking thereby the quiet of the ceremony. We should thoughtfully prepare our gift at home, and not in the spirit with which we respond to an irksome if not presumptuous demand, but in the spirit of a genuine offering, a sacrifice that we really feel. And when we place the money in the basket, let it be with reverence to God and with charity to all.

7

The Sacrifice

When the Sanctus has been spoken and the Canon of the Mass begins, we should remind ourselves: "Now I shall witness, indeed partake in, what the ancient Church called *actio*, the essential act." We must give our full attention to it. As soon as silence reigns once again, we should say to ourselves: "The Lord's last will and testament is being executed. He said: 'As often as you shall do these things, in memory of me shall you do them.'" What happened in the room of the Last Supper is taking place here: Christ comes. He is present in His salutary love and in the destiny that it met. The priest acts, but we must act with him by being inwardly present, by watching him every moment at the altar table, identifying ourselves with his every gesture.

Then comes the Agnus Dei. The priest says the prayer of preparation for Communion and partakes of the sacred food. He then shows the faithful the Host, saying:

"Behold the Lamb of God, behold Him who takes away the sins of the world." And he gives it to those at the Communion rail. Thus another of the Lord's commands is obeyed: "Take ye all and eat this" (1 Cor. 11:24).

The priest acts and we act with him, following observantly, spiritually. Naturally, we must be genuinely active, not simply watchful. We must overcome the unconcern, sleepiness, indolence, and inertia which keep us from the sacred act so that we may enter into it vitally.

Composure alone enables us to do this. When the mind is not collected and the heart is restless and inattentive, the believer will be occasionally conscious of a word or gesture, or the bell will remind him that one of the high points of the Mass is at hand; never will he be in that state of active, watchful vitality which alone permits genuine participation. Liturgical action begins with learning composure. Everything else is important and fruitful only as long as it is rooted in self-collectedness.

Composure and the participation springing from it must be practiced. There is a much-aired opinion that only the prayer and religious act rising involuntarily from within are genuine. This is erroneous. Prayer and religious action are life. But life consists only partly in spontaneous acts; most of life is service and conscious effort, and both are at least as important as impulsive activity.

The Sacrifice

We so often use the phrase *church service*. Service does not imply action overflowing naturally from an inner need, but rather action performed in obedience at the appointed time. When it is service in God's sight rather than man's, it is not only external action but also—and preeminently—inner action, participation. Hence divine serving must be learned and practiced over and over again so that it may become increasingly vigilant, profound, true. Then we shall be granted also that living experience which is beyond all willing and practicing. We shall be seized and so drawn into the act of salvation that we will really exist in the memorial of the Lord, a work not of men, but of God. It is the imperishable reality of the salutary act, God-sent in the hour of the sacred ceremony that enters the world and time ever and again. Consciousness of this divine event is doubtless the greatest gift the Mass can give. It comes, however, only when God gives it. Our task lies in the effort and in loyalty of service.

8

The Altar as Threshold

The real God speaks in the plain, exact words of His messengers through the person, life, and death of Jesus Christ. He challenges the world, arousing it from its captivity, demanding that it recognize the truth and be converted.

The otherness of that conversion is stressed by the fact that the celebration of God's mystery does not take place just anywhere: neither in the spaciousness of nature, nor in the intimacy of a home, but in the unique, clearly circumscribed area of the church. Thus we find the constantly repeated procedure: the believer goes to the house of God, crosses the threshold, and enters the sacred room within. This is an important part of genuine piety. He remains present, listens, speaks, acts, serves.

There is also a special order established within the sacred interior. It is essential to the Liturgy that the important acts of which it is composed are not left to chance or to the momentary spiritual situation, but are arranged and specified with the greatest care. The Lord's memorial sacrifice cannot take place anywhere in the church, but only at one particular spot: the altar.

The altar is a great mystery. Its religious archetype is to be found in almost all faiths; indeed, I doubt that it is fundamentally absent from any. It appears in the Old Testament. In the catacombs we find it in its earliest form. What then is the altar? Its meaning is probably most clearly suggested by two images: it is threshold and it is table.

Threshold is door, and it has a double significance: border and crossing over. It indicates where one thing ends and another begins. The border that marks the end of the old makes possible entry into the new. As a threshold, the altar creates first of all the border between the realm of the world and the realm of God.

The altar reminds us of the remoteness in which He lives beyond the altar, as we might say (meaning "divine distance") or above the altar (meaning "divine loftiness"), both of which are to be understood of course not spatially, but spiritually. They mean that God is the Intangible One, far removed from all approaching, from all grasping; that He is the all-powerful Majestic One immeasurably exalted above earthly things and earthly striving. Such breadth and height are founded not on measure, but on God's essence: His holiness, to which man of himself has no access.

On the other hand, this is not to be understood merely spiritually, or rather, merely intellectually. In the Liturgy everything is symbolic. But symbol is more than a corporal form representing something incorporeal. Let us take, for example, a representation of justice: a woman, blindfolded and holding scales in her hands. The meaning of such a statue is not apparent. First one must be instructed that the bandaged eyes mean that a judge is no respecter of persons; and the scales mean that to each is to be measured out his exact due. This is allegory, whose meaning is not directly perceived.

The Liturgy also contains allegories, but its basic forms are symbols. Their meaning is actually hidden, yet it reveals itself in a particular thing or person, much as the human soul, itself invisible, becomes perceptible, approachable in the expression and movements of a face. So it is in the church. The altar is not an allegory, but a symbol. The thoughtful believer does not have to be taught that it is a border, that above it stretch inaccessible heights and beyond it the reaches of divine remoteness; somehow he is aware of this. To grasp the mystery all that is necessary on the part of the believer is intrinsic readiness and calm reflection; then his heart will respond with reverence.

It is essential for every one of us to experience at some time or another the fear of the Lord, to be repelled by Him from the sacred place, as Moses was at the burning bush (Exod. 3:2-5), that we may know with all our being that God is God and we are but man. Trust in God, nearness to Him, and security in Him remain thin and feeble when personal knowledge of God's exclusive majesty and awful sanctity do not counterbalance them. We do well to pray God for this experience, and the place where it is most likely to be granted us is before His altar.

Threshold is not, however, only borderline; it is also crossing over. One can step over it into the adjacent room or, standing on it, receive Him who comes from the other side. It is something that unites, a place of contact and encounter. This too is contained in the symbol of the altar.

The essence of revelation is the news that God loves us. God's love is not simply the love we find also in ourselves, infinitely intensified. Inconceivable mystery, it had to be revealed: an unheard-of act that we can begin to fathom only when it is clear to us who God is and who we are. Its real expression is to be found in the tremendous event of the Incarnation, when God abandoned His sacred reserve, came to us, became one of us, sharing with us human life and human destiny. Now He is with us, "on our side." Such is His love, and it creates a nearness that man alone never could have conceived.

All this is expressed by the altar. It reminds us that God turns to us; from His heights He steps down to us; from His remoteness He approaches us. The altar is the sign of God's presence among us, in us. The same altar also suggests that there is a way leading us — remote, isolated creatures that we are — back to our Creator; from the depths of our sin up to His holiness; that we can follow it — to be sure, not on our own strength, but on that which His grace supplies. We can cross the border only because God crossed it to come to us. His descent draws us upward. He Himself, the One-Who-Has-Come, is "the way, and the truth, and the life" (John 14:6).

Threshold really lies everywhere in the simple fact that God is Creator and man creature; and this fact is heightened by man's sinfulness, which makes him unable to stand before the Holy God. Yet God has stooped to us in an act of saving love and laid out for us the road to Himself. Thus everywhere we are confronted by sacred barriers repelling us, but also by the possibility of their opening for us. What we call prayer is the mysterious process of that opening.

The Altar as Threshold

Every time we invoke God, we approach His threshold and pass over it. In the altar the barrier presents itself in a form symbolizing God's revelation, for there in the mystery of the Mass it comes to its own in a very special way. Through Christ's self-sacrifice in salutary death, a sacrifice that presupposed the Incarnation of God's Son, the altar-threshold appears most clearly as the borderline that shows who Holy God is and what our sin is. But the altar-threshold is also the crossing-over par excellence, because God became man so that we might become "partakers of the divine nature" (2 Pet. 1:4). The altar is indeed the holy place before which we can say as we can nowhere else: "I am here, O Lord."

9

The Altar as Table

The altar is the threshold to God's immanence. Through Christ, God ceased to be the Unknown, the Inaccessible One. He turned to us, came to us, and became one of us in order that we might go to Him and become one with Him.

The altar is the frontier, the border where God comes to us and we go to Him in a most special manner. But the mystery of the altar is only partially suggested by the image of the threshold; altar is also table.

The presentiment of a sacred table at which not only man but also divinity takes its place is to be found in the religions of all peoples. Everywhere the pious believer places gifts upon an altar so that the godhead may accept them. The idea that these gifts belong to the godhead and no longer to men is conveyed by their destruction or withdrawal from human use. The body of the sacrificial animal is burned, the drink poured out upon the ground.

The Altar as Table

This immolation symbolizes what is contained in the process of death: the passing over to the other side, to the realm of the divine.

A second process is often related to the first. Not everything is given over; part is retained—or rather returned (for what was destroyed represented the whole)—now to be enjoyed by the offerers. Thus godhead and man are nourished by the same sacred food. Indeed, behind this concept lies one still more profound: man's offering stands for himself, is really himself; the true offering is human sacrifice. Again, the offering stands for the godhead itself; true nourishment is divine life.

From a certain standpoint these conceptions are very profound, although closer examination reveals that they have sunk into gloom, worldliness, and animalism. The godhead, then, lives from the life of man—of a tribe, a people; on the other hand, man sees in his godhead the spiritual mainspring of his own life and that of his clan, tribe, people. Divinity has need of man and man of divinity, for in the final analysis they are the same; sacrifice is the constantly renewed process of this union.

Such conceptions are totally absent from the Old Testament. The God to whose altar offerings are brought is neither the vital principle of a people nor the secret of the world's vitality, but Creator and Lord of all that is. The offering is an acknowledgment of His lordship; it in no way affects His potency, but is simply a recognition that all things are His and that man may dispose of them only with His permission. Strictly speaking, the animal from the flock should be slaughtered only before the altar—not because God has any need of its blood, but because all life is His property; the harvest should be consumed only before the altar, since everything that bears its seed "within itself" belongs to God. This idea is expressed in the sacrifice of livestock and in the offering of the fields' firstfruits. Only then does man receive herd and harvest back from the altar for his own use.

The altar is the table to which the heavenly Father invites us. Through salvation we have become sons and daughters of God, and His house is ours. At the altar we enjoy the intimate community of His sacred table. From His hand we receive the "bread of heaven," the word of truth, and—far excelling all imaginable gifts—His own incarnate Son, the living Christ (see John 6). What is given us, then, is at once corporal reality and sentient truth, Life and Person—in short, Gift.

But if we ask whether at the sacred table God too receives something, whether the age-old presentiment of a real community of table between God and man is not also fulfilled in the clean air of Christian faith, the answer is not easy. Fear of being irreverent makes us cautious. However, we can point to a mystery that fills the letters of St. Paul and appears also in the farewell speeches of St. John's Gospel. The fruit of the divine sojourn on earth is salvation. This means not only our forgiveness and justification but also that the world is brought home to the Father. And again, not only in the sense that we return to God in love and obedience but that men are received into divine life—and through men, the world in all its reality. God desires this. When we are told that He loves us, this does not mean that He is merely benevolent toward us; the word is meant in all its abundance.

God longs for men. He wants to have His creatures close to Him. When Christ cried from the Cross, "I thirst" (John 19:28), a dying man's bodily torment was indeed expressed, but much more besides.

Similarly at Jacob's well, when the disciples encouraged Jesus to eat the food they had brought, He replied: "My food is to do the will of Him who sent me, to accomplish His work" (John 4:34). Mysterious hungering and thirsting this—the hunger and thirst of God! St. Augustine writes that receiving the Eucharist does not so much mean that we partake of the divine life offered us, as that the divine life draws us into itself. These thoughts should not be pressed too far, for they are holy. It is important, however, to know that a mystery of divine-human love and communion does exist and that it is realized at the altar.

10

Holy Day

The holy place, set apart from the rest of the world, came into being when God's Son appeared on earth: when He was conceived in Nazareth, born in Bethlehem, lived among us in Palestine—and in such a manner that it could be said: "There He is; there He goes." Is there perhaps a holy time as well?

Again it is a question of a time not of man's making. There exists no deed, no experience, no dedication by which man of himself can so sanctify a day or an hour that it becomes holy in God's sight. God alone can sanctify a period of time by personally entering into it. I am in time because I live and unfold in time, act in it, experience destiny; but are such things conceivable of God? Our answer is spontaneous: "No." God lives not only forever, but eternally; His life has nothing to do with time. He neither grows nor declines, develops nor changes—all that would involve time—but realizes His infinite essence wholly and perfectly in purest actuality. He did create time, as He created everything else that exists; more correctly, He created the world, which exists in time. Thus He is present in all time, in its smallest as in its largest fraction. God fills them all, and no one period is holier than another. What is decisive is whether the universally governing sanctity of God is able to step to the fore in a specific instance, moving men and engraving itself into the historical memory.

We are not concerned here with the problem just stated. Such a holy hour could appear at any time: in the evolution of nature, in the relations between members of a family, in history. When the Liturgy speaks of sacred time it means something specific, similar to the specificity of the sacred place. What it is, however, only Revelation can say. And it does say, with all clarity: one of the seven days of the week is sacred to God, the day on which He "rested" after creating the universe.

The message given us by Revelation is meant to be taken realistically. It signifies something mysterious, yes, but also something explicit. In the book of Genesis, God's handiwork is described as being completed in the course of a week. Six days long God creates; on the seventh He rests. The biblical report has nothing to do with the question, "When—in what period—did the stars, plants, animals come into existence?" *Week* does not signify a period of time in the ordinary sense of the word; it is rather a symbol for the wise, humanly intelligible order in which creation took place. But over and above this, the word *week* means something very precise: from the earliest beginnings of the world God arranged its seven days in such a fashion as to allow man six for his work; the seventh, however, He reserved for Himself, setting it apart because "on this day," having completed creation, He entered into His rest.

The sacredness of the Lord's Day is due not to any experience of man—however holy—but to God and to His resting on that day. Or to put it more precisely, there exists for God in connection with creation a mystery known as "divine repose." We cannot understand it—what could it possibly mean, rest for the Omnipotent? When we accept this mystery on faith, however, we do sense the presence of something very profound.

God is not only the eternal Spirit who is spoken of in philosophical absolutes; He is also the Acting One, of whom it may be said that He decides, that He rises, creates, forms, arranges, and that He rests.

It is this mystery of God's rest that permeates the seventh day of the week, as the others are permeated by the mystery of divine activity. Sunday has an almost sacramental character. In the sacrament, a natural process, like that of bathing or of confessing one's guilt is related to the governing of grace. During the natural act, supernatural grace becomes effective, much as the movements of the soul activate the body. Something similar is to be found in the mystery of the Sabbath.

The natural tension caused by six days of work and its slackening on the day of rest create the form into which God has sunk the mystery of His repose in order to convey it to us. To keep the Sabbath is to become aware of the mystery of divine rest, to revere it, and to express it in our arrangement of the day.

Precisely because Sunday is not a product of the natural life-rhythm, it is vulnerable. The merely natural somehow manages to assert itself; the roots of Sunday, however, lie in revelation. Thus it is easily destroyed, in spite of the important natural need which it also meets. Other considerations—economic, social, or what have you—constantly shove it aside. Work gnaws at it; amusement elbows its way into it, crowding out holiness; the significance of keeping holy is itself misunderstood, and rest is imposed with a resultant boredom that is worse than if work had continued.

Sunday, then, poses a real problem, which each of us must solve according to his own particular circumstances.

Holy Day

The day is important for the individual, but above all for the family. We must understand what is at stake, realize its value for us, and tackle the problem as energetically and as wholeheartedly as we do other matters important to us.

11

The Holy Day and the Sacred Hour

"And so the heavens and the earth were finished, and all the furniture of them. And on the seventh day God ended His work which He had made; and He rested on the seventh day from all His work which He had done. And He blessed the seventh day, and sanctified it: because in it He had rested from all His work which God created and made" (Gen. 2:1-3). The seventh day, the Sabbath. The holy day of the New Testament, however, is Sunday, the first day of the week.

Here again something typical of the New Testament has occurred. Jesus Christ was the Executant of the Old Testament but its Lord as well. In Him the promise of the coming Messiah, which gleams throughout the Old Testament, is fulfilled. With Christ's death and Resurrection the new order began. The evening before His death, while establishing the Eucharist, Jesus spoke with divine simplicity of the "new covenant in my blood" (Luke 22:20).

The Holy Day and the Sacred Hour

The day of Easter, on which He rose again, crowning His mission, now becomes the new day of completion. Again God rests from His work of creation—this time the creation from which the new man, the new heaven and earth are supposed to emerge. This day returns every week as Sunday, a memorial of the first creation's wedding with the second. The divine repose of the Sabbath now mingles with the triumph of the Resurrection. Into the hum of peace breaks the fanfare of victory. Promise and fulfillment have become one. For the Sabbath looked back—in eternity—to the beginning. Sunday looks forward—in eternity—to the end, to what is to come. It has an eschatological character. It proclaims Christ's new creation, the new world born of His deed and one day to be revealed in eternity.

We asked whether it is possible to speak of God's resting, since He is He Who Is, the Omnipotent One, eternal, unchanging; revelation replies that He truly makes decisions; He creates; and He rests from creating. This double aspect of the all-pervasive, all-governing God who is yet personally free to come and go and act in a specific instance is proclaimed throughout Scripture. The Bible recounts His selection of a particular person, His sealing a covenant of loyalty with him, His consolidation of that covenant with the nation that grew from the chosen man's descendants, His divine guidance and support in their constant struggles against their own inertia and stubbornness, His never-failing loyalty, His rescuing them from repeated apostasy. Again and again God experiences the lot of magnanimity betrayed. The account goes on to tell how He then revealed Himself in all His reality: the Father sends His eternal Son into the world as the long-awaited Messiah. The Holy Spirit governs that entire life, and everyone is aware of its unheard-of power. Finally, God's Son, accepting with supreme readiness the fate prepared for Him among men, allows the storm-clouds of centuries-old opposition to the divine to gather and break over His head and slay Him. The completion of this act on Calvary, the victory of the Resurrection, is expressed in the day of the Lord.

But God's lot among men finds another expression in time—namely, in the Mass itself.

The *Gottesschicksal*, or divine fate, took place in time. As divine act and fate, however, it issued from the divine will. It took place once as an earthly event with beginning and end. Simultaneously it is an unchanging reality in eternity. There Christ stands with His Passion and death before the Father. Before He died He willed that this salutary fulfillment be constantly remembered. At the Last Supper He gave His friends the bread of His body and the wine of His blood, exhorting them to "do this" in His memory. As often as those authorized to do so obey this command, what occurred then occurs again — in the present. The memorial is no mere recollection; it is a return to actual being. Through the act of the Lord's memorial, the eternal reality of God's earthly destiny, renewed ever and again, steps into time. This entry is the holy hour, the constantly recurring now. It is not as though there existed one hour which man reserves for his God; God Himself, bearing His salutary destiny, enters into the hour, which attains self-realization through Him. It now becomes part of the new creation. Through such an hour, time contains eternity, and eternity embraces time.

When the eternal God took upon Himself our human transitoriness, sacred time in the real sense of the words came into being. At first that was simply the time that lay between the angel's annunciation and the Lord's departure. Within those years the incarnate Son of God lived, worked, and suffered among us — then and only then. During the reign of Caesar Augustus, God really became man, and while Pontius Pilate was procurator of Judea He really died — not sooner, not later. Between those two events the eternal Logos existed as a man. This earthly sojourn is renewed in the Mass. When the priest, empowered by the Lord Himself, speaks the words over the bread and the wine, Christ walks alive and real among His congregation until He gives Himself as nourishment in the sacred Supper. Again a definite span of time with beginning and end: the Passover of the Lord in the most literal sense of the phrase.

To participate properly in the Mass it is essential that we be aware of its temporalness: of its beginning, continuation, and end. This brief portion of time enfolds eternity. Customs like that of exposing the Blessed Sacrament during the Mass can blur the sense of sacred temporalness in the Mass. The constant figure of the host, starlike above the altar, cancels the sense of the Lord's coming, pausing, and departing.

It is very important to experience the pass-over of the sacred moment emerging from eternity. It catches us up into itself, and while it lasts we are different from what we are at all other times. Then it dismisses us, and we fall back into the transitoriness of day-to-day existence. But if we have vitally participated in it, we take with us the seed of that holy eternity which comes from the Resurrection, and our life in the transitory world is changed.

12

The Sacred Act

A religious act can have various origins. What we desire most today is immediate experience.

Let us suppose that a group of people has just been rescued from mortal danger. It is not difficult to imagine that in response to some inner urge they grow still, remove their hats, or make some other earnest gesture of reverence and gratitude to God. Their act would be a direct expression of their experience, possible only at that moment and for those particular people. Were it to be repeated, it would at once become artificial and embarrassing.

The act could also spring from the consciousness of a significant, regularly recurring hour: for instance, after the labor, encounters, and providential experiences of the day, before man enters upon the darkness of sleep, which heralds death's long night. At this moment his impulse is to pause, to collect and place himself in the hands of his

Maker; and if he has learned to heed such inner prompt-ings, he will do so. With the beginning of the day comes a similar impulse. Then, too, man is conscious of the need to do something religious, to become established in him-self and turn to face what God expects of him during the coming day. At the close of the old year and the open-ing of the new, such an impulse, intensified, also makes itself felt. Acts of this kind are repeatable, even under varying circumstances and by different people; for they spring, not from a unique experience, but from the recur-rent rhythms of existence.

Finally, a religious act can also be instituted. That is, some act can be made valid and obligatory. Only he who possesses authority can institute with genuine validity. God did so during the Exodus from Egypt, when He com-manded that the liberation be annually commemorated in the feast of the Passover.

It was during this commemoration, at the Last Supper, that Christ instituted a second commemoration, that of His death. His oneness with the Father's will, His life and salutary destiny, His living, messianic reality—all are expressed in the words spoken over the bread and wine and in the common partaking of the sacred food. And He instructed His followers to repeat it forever: "As often as you shall do these things, in memory of me shall you do them." This is institution par excellence, the core of Christian divine service.

When God established the law of the Passover, He instructed the people to offer sacrifice on a certain day, celebrating together a feast commemorating their former liberation from Egypt. This act, which emerged from the humanly possible, received its real significance from divine direction.

The act Christ instituted is different. He did not say: "On a certain day of the year you are to come together and share a meal in friendship. Then shall the eldest bless bread and wine and invoke my memory." Such an act would be similar to the Passover, issuing from the humanly possible; only the event it was celebrating would be divine.

Christ spoke differently. His "do these things" implies "things I have just done"; yet what He did surpasses human possibility. It is an act of God springing as incomprehensibly from His love and omnipotence as the acts of Creation or the Incarnation. And such an act He entrusts to men! He does not say: "Pray God to do thus," but simply "do." Thus He places in human hands an act that can be fulfilled only by the divine. Its mystery is similar to that of sacred time and place, already discussed. Man acts; but in his human action is the act of God. And not only in the general sense that God is present in all human endeavor because all our reality and strength, wisdom and will come from Him. This is a specific, historical act; here the word *institution* has a special, unique significance. God determined, proclaimed, and instituted; man is to execute the act. When he does so, God makes of it something of which He alone is capable.

Subject to the divine nature of the act is a certain human attitude, a certain indispensable bearing. If something of the origin and freshness of the experience is to be transmitted, the individual must be aware of what is happening and have the vigor to express it. Its expression must be credible, vital, genuine, powerful in word and gesture. If the act is to be related significantly to regularly returning hours or seasons, the participant must feel the truth of the relation and of the mystery behind it. He must have an expression for it that remains valid through all the variations of the hours.

For the institutional act one other thing is necessary: not creative experience and repeatable expression, not the constantly renewed realization of its existential significance in our lives, but obedience to the will of the Institutor. It is for men to hear the Lord and to do as He commands. It is service in faith and obedience. It is not an independent human act but acceptance of a divine undertaking that prepares a place for it, shapes for it a body of earthly cooperation. In the profoundest sense of the word it is a selfless act whereby man arrives at his true self. That is why the act of the Mass can be renewed time and again under the most varied circumstances of general as well as personal history, in hours of spiritual abundance and of spiritual need, in affliction and mourning or in freedom and joy.

13

The Executory Word

The word of God permeates the whole of the Mass, as it also fills the entire Liturgy. Some of its parts (such as the Epistle and the Gospel or the Our Father), spoken at the most solemn moments, are larger unbroken passages which have been taken bodily from Scripture. The Introit, the Offertory, and the Collects consist of sentences selected from various biblical books to highlight the significance of the day in question. The same is true of the Gradual and the Tract, texts that link the Epistle and the Gospel. Finally, in the actual prayers, words from, or references to, the preceding scriptural quotations return again and again to fortify the whole with their sacred power.

At the heart of the Mass—the Consecration—the word of the Lord assumes a special character. Following the Offertory, in which bread and wine are prepared for the sacred feast, is the most important prayer of all: the Canon of the Mass.

The Executory Word

After the *Quam oblationem*, the Church's final prayer over the gift-offerings, we have the words:

Who, the day before He suffered, took bread into His holy and venerable hands, and with His eyes lifted up to heaven, unto Thee, God, His almighty Father, giving thanks to Thee, He blessed, broke and gave it to His disciples, saying: Take and eat ye all of this, for this is my body. In like manner, after He had supped, taking also this excellent chalice into His holy and venerable hands, and giving thanks to Thee, He blessed and gave it to His disciples, saying: Take and drink ye all of this, for this is the chalice of my blood, of the new and eternal testament: the mystery of faith: which shall be shed for you and for many unto the remission of sins. As often as you shall do these things, ye shall do them in remembrance of me.

The words are taken from the Gospel reports and from the first letter to the Corinthians. Like the original letter and Gospel texts, they seem to repeat, only more impressively, what took place at that time.

But when we look closely, we notice slight shifts in the wording. Not only does the priest, by reading the biblical account, relate what took place; he also does it himself.

His words are no longer merely the biblical "and giving thanks"; they have become: "and with His eyes lifted up to heaven, unto Thee, God, His almighty Father, giving thanks to Thee." God is actually being addressed. And while the priest says "took bread," he actually picks up the Host lying there, bowing his head at the word *thanks*. Thus the decisive sentences, *"for this is my body"* and *"for this is the chalice of my blood, of the new and eternal testament: the mystery of faith: which shall be shed for you and for many unto the remission of sins,"* acquire a new character.

The whole passage moves from the past into the present, from the report to the act. It is no longer a pious memorial; it has become a living reality. At the Consecration of the chalice we were being prepared for something extraordinary: *mysterium fidei*. In the early Church, while the priest softly spoke the words which established the Eucharist, the deacon raised his voice and reverently called out: "Take heed! The mystery of faith!" It is in this sense that we must receive the Lord's words. But the full significance of their springing into life is clearest in the final sentence: "As often as ye shall do these things, ye shall do them in remembrance of me."

Here again something happens to the scriptural word that does not happen to the Epistle or Gospel, to the Our Father or the praises of the Gloria. There God's biblical words are read, proclaimed, and heard; priest and people make them their own and pass them back as prayer to God. Here the word becomes the living present. What was once spoken by Christ is spoken anew, not as a new word issuing from the hour and consequently passing away with it, but as the old, Christ-spoken word renewed and become part of this hour.

We are about to anticipate, but the point to be discussed in detail later is so all important that it can bear repetition. What Jesus accomplished by these words differed from all the other proofs of His divine omnipotence. Not only was He summoning the powers of creation to the service of the kingdom of God; here, as in the Incarnation and the Resurrection, He was laying the foundations of a new creation.

These words are the equals of those which once brought the universe into existence. But it was the Lord's pleasure to permit them their creative task not only once, the evening He spoke them, but from henceforth forever—or, as St. Paul says, "until He comes" (1 Cor. 11:26). They are meant to ring out ever and again in the course of history, accomplishing each time what they first effected. To this end Christ gave them to His followers with the command: "As often as ye shall do these things, ye shall do them in remembrance of me" (Luke 22:20).

Therefore when the priest utters the words, they are not merely reported; they rise and create. Obviously, at this point we do not simply hear a man talking. The priest pronounces the words, certainly; but they are not his. He is only their bearer; and he does not bear them by reason of his personal faith or piety or moral strength, but by means of his office, through which he executes the Lord's directions. The true speaker remains Christ. He alone can speak thus. The priest merely lends the Lord his voice, mind, will, and freedom, playing a role similar to that of the baptismal water, for the new birth is not brought about by its natural cleansing qualities, but by the power of Christ. It is Christ who baptizes, just as here it is Christ who speaks.

Our own attitude should be in keeping with this. It is not merely a question of pious listening and acceptance, nor is it one of consummation in the literal sense of the word. The first would be too little; the second definitely too much. The deacon's interjection in the midst of the holy sentences gives us the right cue: *mysterium fidei!* The call proclaims the unfolding of the inmost earnestness, the supreme love of God, summoning us to muster all the readiness and power of our faith in order to participate in them.

14

The Word of Praise

Prayer appears in Holy Mass primarily in the impressive form of praise or hymn. Such is the greater doxology or chant of honor, called the Gloria after its opening word. It begins with the praise of the angels over Bethlehem (Luke 2:14), continues with expressions lauding God's glory, then shifts to a kind of litany in which the all-holy Persons of the divine Trinity—above all, Christ—are supplicated, and ends with the solemn naming of the threefold God.

The part of the Mass known as the Preface is also praise. This introduces the most important prayer of the Mass, the Canon, which includes the Consecration. Indicative of the solemnity of the Preface are its introductory sentences with which priest and people alternately stimulate and strengthen each other's spiritual exaltation. The hymn proper then begins with homage to the Father in heaven, homage based each time on the particular mystery of the feast that is being celebrated.

After joining in the glorious praises of the angel choirs, it terminates with the adoration of the Sanctus. The first part of this prayer is taken from the vision of the prophet Isaiah, who heard it from the lips of the cherubim (Isa. 6:3); the second is from the Gospel passage describing Jesus' entry into Jerusalem, where the exulting children shouted the words to Him in the streets (Matt. 21:9).

On certain feast days we find further praises, called Sequences, tucked between Epistle and the Gospel. They are hymnal proclamations of the feast's central event, through which they appeal to God. Sequences are to be found mainly in the Masses of Easter, Pentecost, and Corpus Christi.

Sometimes praise, common also in the Graduals, breaks into certain forms of the Introit, Offertory, and Collects (prayers briefly interspersed with *alleluias*) which are entwined about Epistle and Gospel. These praises continue the themes of the Psalms and songs of praise in the Old and New Testaments: inspired man, brimming with the experience of God's grandeur, glory, and awesomeness, with His love and His fervor, proclaims God's omnipotence, admiring, lauding, and worshipping Him. The praise-giver lives in this glory as in a special atmosphere in which he delights. In praise man's prayer is farthest removed from the everyday world.

The Word of Praise

This sense of the heights is particularly apparent in the prelude to the Preface, in which priest and congregation help each other to leave behind them everything low and mean and to ascend. First they wish each other God's strength: "The Lord be with you," prays the priest, to which the people reply: "And with thy spirit." God is asked to move and fortify His people, to accompany the spirit of His priest. Spirit here is not intellect, but that simultaneous intimacy and exaltation from which the movements of love, adoration, and enthusiasm climb.

Then the priest calls: "Lift up your hearts." The congregation responds: "We have lifted them up unto the Lord." To this comes the new summons: "Let us give thanks to the Lord our God." Response: "It is meet and just." Linked to the last word is the Preface itself: "It is truly meet and just, right and availing unto salvation, that we should at all times and in all places give thanks unto Thee, O holy Lord, Father almighty and everlasting God."

In these lines something peculiar to the prayer of praise is particularly apparent: thanksgiving. It is a rendering of thanks not for some beautiful or useful gift, but for the whole of blessed existence. It is man's response to the glory of God unveiled by revelation, man's response to His "Epiphany."

Man thanks his Creator for everything, for everything is His gift: natural life, the gift of creation; supernatural life, that of salvation. Such thanksgiving finds its most beautiful expression in the Gloria: "*Gratias agimus tibi propter magnam gloriam tuam.*" "*Gratias agere*" means "to thank, to honor, to wish well." Greeks and Romans particularly praised the virtue of magnanimity, the free nobility of being. This attitude appears here in relation to God: "We give thee thanks for Thy great glory."

Even in human relationships the feeling exists: "I thank you, not for what you have done for me or for what you think of me, but for yourself, for existing." Here love reaches a mysterious greatness. Actually, thanks for the existence of a loved one should be directed elsewhere: to his parents or to God. What seems folly—albeit beautiful folly—is, when applied to God, pure sense, for He exists of Himself. He is the "I am" (Exod. 3:14). Of all existences, His alone has "merit," for it is the perfect expression of His love. For this love, man, shaken by God's glory, thanks Him.

Deep emotion streams through the songs of praise, emotion different from that of personal experience. Its bearer is not the individual, but the whole, the Church. The Church is more than the sum of her believers, more than the huge *ordo* which enfolds them all. Saints Paul and John tell us what she is: a mighty organism, humanity reborn in the Mystical Body of Christ, in which the individual believers are the pulsing cells. It is then the Church who speaks in her great hymns.

One might even venture to say that the joy they voice is not hers alone, but is shared by God Himself. Doesn't St. Paul say that the Holy Spirit Himself pleads for us "with unutterable groanings" (Rom. 8:26)? If this is true of all prayer, then certainly of the prayer of praise. The psalms of the Old Testament stream from prophetic enthusiasm; those of the New from the fire of Pentecost. The Acts of the Apostles and the first letter to the Corinthians testify to the power of that streaming and storming of the Spirit — so powerful that it shattered the order of thought and speech, so that only a stammering and exclaiming could be recognized. The same Paul, however, admonishes men to restrain such outbursts. Higher than storm and stammer sings the clear word controlled by truth and inner discipline, and the faithful should channel their enthusiasm into "spiritual songs" (1 Cor. 12; Eph. 5:19). From these spring the hymns of the Church. The joy and elation of the spirit which the Father sends us in Christ's name break through and return to the Father. This sense of sacred mounting beats like wings through the hymn sung at the consecration of the paschal candle on Easter

Saturday, the *Exultet*, but it is also perceptible in the Gloria and in other songs of praise.

It would be a good preparation for Holy Mass to go over the Gloria or a Gradual or Preface the day before, or before the service begins, to enable these to come alive for us and to allow us to recognize and practice the exaltation that each contains.

15

The Word of Entreaty

In singular contrast to the prayer of praise stands the prayer of entreaty. We find it chiefly in three places: after the Gloria in the Collects, after the Offertory in the Secret, and after the Communion prayer in the Postcommunion. It also appears in the Canon (in the various requests before and after the Consecration) and at the end of the Our Father. Our concern here is with the prayers which appear in the three places mentioned first: the Collect, the Secret, and the Postcommunion.

That they are important is at once seen from the words and gestures which precede them. The priest kisses the altar, an expression of closest contact with the place of God's proximity; then he turns to the people and with a grave and formal gesture says: "The Lord be with you." To this the congregation or server replies: "And with thy spirit." These are the same words of collectedness and strengthening we met earlier in the Preface. The priest says: "*Oremus*—let us pray." And the Collect follows. The preamble of the Secret is even more solemn. There the priest says first: "*Orate, fratres*—Pray, brethren," and then he continues: "that my sacrifice and yours may be acceptable to God the Father almighty." The server answers: "May the Lord receive the Sacrifice at thy hands, to the praise and glory of His name, to our own benefit, and to that of all His holy Church." After this preparation the priest prays over the offerings lying on the altar.

In all these prayers we are struck by one thing: their strict formality. They are terse and austere, the more so the older they are. Here are no elaborate thoughts, no moving images, no emotional outpourings. Nothing but a few clear, terse sentences.

An example is found in the Collect for the first Monday in Lent: "Convert us, O God our salvation; and that the Lenten fast may be of profit to us, instruct our minds with heavenly discipline." And the Secret from the same Mass: "Sanctify, O Lord, the gifts offered to Thee: and cleanse us from the stains of our sins." Finally the Postcommunion: "Filled with the gift of Thy salvation, we humbly beseech Thee, O Lord, that even as we rejoice in the participation thereof, we may be renewed also by its effect."

The tone seems at first foreign to us. Our prayers are usually wordier. There is more emotion in them, and they are far more personal. Of course, not all the prayers of the Mass are as austere as these, which have come down to us from a very early period, but their general tenor is more or less the same. The more subjective prayer is always of a later origin and somehow has lost its reserve.

The early prayers spring not from the personal experience of the individual, but from the consciousness of the congregation or, more exactly, of the Church. Often they are very official, in the original sense of the word: the outcome of the *officium*, duty, the charges of office. Roman clarity and objectivity so dominate them that to us of another stamp and era they often seem cool and impersonal — perhaps even unreligious. But in this we should be very much mistaken, for they are packed with a piety both powerful and profound.

We cannot grasp the significance of these texts without real effort. They are the fruit of deep concentration. An alert sense of reality has experienced life; an unclouded mind has recognized and seized upon the essential; precise and telling expression has made possible their complete simplicity. The history of the first centuries best reveals the masterly grasp of reality that forms the basis of these prayers; for the young Church had to struggle heroically, first with the voluptuous luxury of a decaying antiquity, then with the mighty forces that came into existence in the chaos of the great migrations and of the dawning Middle Ages.

They are not, as we might suppose, complete self-explanatory texts; the situation from which they spring was summed up in the silent prayers that preceded them. We do not take the introductory "Let us pray" seriously enough.

The procedure really should be as follows: Folding his hands, the priest says: "*Oremus* — let us pray." Now there is silence for a good while, during which the individual believer, taking the mystery of the day as his theme, prays for his own intention and for the intention of the congregation. This silent, manifold praying is then gathered up by the priest and expressed in the few sentences of the Collect, so that its brief words are filled with all the vitality that has just silently lifted itself to God. Now its terseness no longer seems inadequate, but rich and recapitulative. By studying the Collects beforehand, we could make them the vehicles of our intentions, as they were meant to be.

These prayers are significant for the direction which prayer takes in them. The catechism defines prayer as a lifting of the heart to God, for God is above us and our way to Him leads upwards. He is also in us; so the way to Him leads through the inner sanctuary. How does this movement take place? Has it some guiding principle or method?

All Collects, regardless of content, close with a remarkable sentence: "Through our Lord Jesus Christ, who livest and reignest with God the Father in the unity of the Holy Spirit, God, world without end." Here is the direction we were seeking, the proper relation between the goal, the way, and the power which enables us to take it. The goal is the Father; prayer is a seeking of His face. "The Way" is Christ. The power is the Holy Spirit. This one sentence contains the whole law of liturgical prayer. Its method is the same used by the divine Trinity in the work of our salvation. All things come from and return to the Father. In the Logos, He created the world. When man sinned, Christ was sent into the world to rescue it and restore it to the Father. The power by which the eternal Son became man and fulfilled His task was that of the Holy Spirit. In the strength of this same Spirit, sent us by the Father in the Son's name, we return along the road of Christ home to the Father. We are Christians in Christ. Our new life is life-in-Him. Hence Christian prayer is prayer in Christ.

By this time the attentive reader will have noticed that almost invariably the Liturgy unrolls before the Father, to whom all words and acts are addressed. Very rarely, and then only for an obvious reason, does it turn to the Son: for instance in the Gloria, where one of the holy Persons after the other is invoked, or in the Agnus Dei, as the priest's eyes seem to meet those of the Savior offering Himself for sacrifice.

The prayers of later periods are more inclined to address themselves to Christ, but we feel at once that somehow they are out of order. The holy Countenance to which the words of the Liturgy are directed is that of the Father; but at every point Christ is the vital room in which everything takes place and the Way that is taken. His Revelation is the Truth that meets us wherever we look. His living, dying, and rising again is the power that lifts all things into newness. His living reality is the model for, and the manner of, holy existence, the essential to which we should surrender ourselves and in which we should exist. The Holy Spirit is the power by which we are meant to accomplish both the oneness with Christ and the movement toward the Father.

16

The Congregation
and Injustice Rectified

The word *congregation* does not mean "a gathering of many people"—not even of many pious and reverent people. Even in such a group that unifying, simultaneously fortifying and fervent quality which is the essence of the true congregation might be lacking. Christ defines it: "For where two or three are gathered together for my sake, there am I in the midst of them" (Matt. 18:20). The Acts of the Apostles gives more details in its report on the days following Pentecost: "And continuing daily with one accord in the temple, and breaking bread in their houses, they took their food with gladness and simplicity of heart, praising God and being in favor with all the people" (Acts 2:46-47). A congregation, then, exists when a number of people disciplined by faith and conscious of their membership in Christ gather to celebrate the sacred mysteries. Even then it does not follow effortlessly. There are a few exceptions when it does seem to—for instance, when an oppressive need or powerful joy spontaneously fills and fuses all hearts; or when the words of an inspired teacher have moved the hearers to genuine Christian *unitas*, making of the many individuals one great body drawn by the same power to the same end. But as a rule congregation exists only when its members will it.

Many things can help: the solemnity of the room, organ music, the power of the Divine Word, the earnestness and mystery of the sacred ceremony. But these can only help; they cannot do everything. From the standpoint of our personal responsibility, they are unable to achieve even the main thing. For a congregation must be possible also without these: in uninspiring surroundings; with the feeblest music or none at all; with the sacred word inadequately proclaimed; a divine service to which all possible human shortcomings cling. Above all, if there is to be a congregation, the believers must know what a congregation is; they must desire it and actively strive to attain it.

In the Sermon on the Mount, the Lord says: "Therefore, if thou art offering thy gift at the altar, and there rememberest that thy brother has anything against thee, leave thy gift before the altar and go first to be reconciled to thy brother, and then come and offer thy gift" (Matt.

5:23-24). This means: When you go to Mass and you recall that you have been unjust to someone and that he bears you a grudge, you cannot simply walk into church as though nothing were wrong. For then you would be entering only the physical room of the building, not the congregation, which would not receive you, as you would destroy it by your mere presence.

A congregation is the sacred coherence that links person to person as it links God to men and men to God. It is the unity of men in Christ; in the living Christ "in the midst of them," before the countenance of His Father, in the efficacy of the Holy Spirit. But if you have wronged your "brother," and he has a grudge against you, a wall rises between you and him that excludes you from the sacred unity; then, as far as you are concerned, congregation ceases to exist. It is your responsibility to restore it by removing the impediment between you and your brother.

You cannot very well go about it as the Sermon on the Mount in its divine simplicity advises: simply by dropping everything, going to the one you have wronged and rectifying things, then returning. Perhaps we should not be so hasty with our "cannots." We can do much more than we suppose, and our watered-down Christian existence would be strengthened if we would more often act with the directness of the believing heart, would simply go and do what love and repentance and magnanimity dictate. I am not lauding impulsiveness; I am only trying to suggest that reflection is sometimes a hindrance, and that often the necessary, truly liberating act is possible only through the power and momentum of the first impulse.

Be this as it may, anyone who knows that somewhere someone has something against him certainly can do one thing: he can promise himself to remove the injustice by correcting it as soon as possible. The honest intention suffices to bring down the wall between himself and his "brother." Immediately the unifying element is free again to contact all parts. As soon as the injustice that isolates has been overcome, the congregation is restored.

Jesus' word can also be reversed. We can say: "Therefore, if thou art offering thy gift at the altar, and there rememberest that thou hast anything against thy brother, leave thy gifts before the altar and go first to be reconciled to thy brother, and then come and offer thy gift." Here you are the one with the complaint. Now you can act much more directly. For the essential depends not on the actual agreement reached by the estranged parties, but on one condition: your forgiveness. As long as you bear your grudge, no matter how "valid," there can be no true congregation as far as you are concerned. Forgive, honestly and sincerely, and the sacred unifying circle will close again. Perhaps this is impossible all at once. Sometimes disappointment and revolt are too great to permit genuine forgiveness right away. Then forgive as much as is in your power and ask God to give you an increase of forgiveness.

For it is not man who effects true forgiveness. The commandment to forgive one's enemies might have been expressed: "Know that thou canst forgive thy enemy because Christ on the Cross forgave His; it is He who effects forgiveness in thee."

So human forgiveness is different from that which the Lord meant. It could be mere prudence, which says, "Let it go—nothing will come of it anyway"; or indifference: "What does it matter?"; or false friendliness, which is no more than inverted dislike; or cowardice, which does not trust itself to fight it out, and so forth. The forgiveness of Christ is different. It means that divine love gains a footing in us, creating that new order which is meant to reign among the sons and daughters of God. Hence when you try to fulfill the law of love for the sake of God and His holy mysteries, you make it possible for God to allow the congregation of those rooted in His love to flower.

17

The Congregation and the Church

When churchgoers enter the sacred precincts, they come as individuals, each with his particular talents and circumstances, worries and wishes. Let us try to get an idea of the kind of life that is pouring into the church. We have a roomful of people, each with his private thoughts, feelings, aims: a conglomeration of little separate worlds. The bearing of everyone present seems to say "I" or at best the "we" of his closest associations: his family, friends, dependents. But even this inclusion often really means little more than a widened self-esteem. The singular ego is stretched to a natural group-ego that is still far removed from genuine congregation.

The true congregation is a gathering of those who belong to Christ, the holy people of God, united by faith and love. Essentially, it is of His making, a piece of new creation, which finds expression in the bearing of its participants.

The Congregation and the Church

When we read the prayers of the Mass with this in mind, we notice that the word *I* appears very seldom and never without a special reason. It is found quite clearly in the prayers at the foot of the altar when each one present acknowledges his sins; in the Credo, when the individual, conscious of his personal responsibility, professes his belief in divine revelation; in the prayers immediately preceding Holy Communion. As a rule, *we* is used: we praise thee, we glorify thee, we adore thee; forgive us, help us, enlighten us. This *we* is not spontaneous, but the carefully nurtured fruit of genuine congregation.

The real antonym of community is not the individual and his individualism, but the egoist and his selfishness. It is this that must first be overcome—and not by frequent or prolonged association, but by mastering the mind and will, which alone allows us to see others as they really are: to acknowledge and accept them; to make their desires and anxieties our own; to restrain ourselves for their sakes.

But to do this we must have solitude, for only in solitude do we have a chance to see ourselves objectively and to free ourselves from our own chains. Someday, perhaps on some special occasion, we will realize what walls of indifference, disregard, enmity loom between us and the other man, and before Mass or during the Introit we will make a real effort to break through them. We will remind ourselves: together we face God; together we are congregation. Not only I and others in general, but this man, that woman over there, and the believer next to me. In God's sight they are all as important as I am—perhaps much more so: purer, braver, less selfish, nobler, more loving and fervent. Among them are perhaps great and holy souls with whom I am fortunate to find myself associated, because the surge of their prayers sweeps me along with it to God!

Then we will let the other believers into the inner circle of our lives, present ourselves to God with them, linking our intentions to theirs. We will consciously, earnestly pray the *we* of the Liturgy, for from such things congregation is formed.

Until now we have spoken of congregation as the Christian *we* in its encounter with God, the community of those united by the same faith and by mutual love. But this is not all. The conception must include also those outside any particular building, even outside the church; for congregation reaches far beyond.

It is no closed circle, no organization or union with its own center. Each congregation is part of a whole that far surpasses any Sunday gathering; it embraces everyone who believes in Christ in the same city, the same country, over the whole earth. The congregation gathered in any one church is influenced by its particular circumstances, by its services, by the quality of its members, and by the particular feasts that they are celebrating. It is a unit, but one that remains open; and all who are bound to Christ are included in it.

Its center is the altar, every altar in every church — altar that is simultaneously the center of the world. At Christ's table all the faithful are remembered, and all belong to the *we* that is spoken there.

And still we have not touched bottom. In the Confiteor priest and the faithful confess their sins. Their confession is addressed primarily to God, and in His presence alternately to each other, but it is also addressed to Mary, the Mother of the Lord, to the archangel Michael, to John the Baptist and the apostles Peter and Paul, and to all the saints. Behind the archangel, who appears here as the leader of the heavenly hosts, stands the world of the angels; and "the saints" means not only the great historical figures of sanctity which the word usually suggests, but all the saved, all who have gone home to God. In other parts of the Mass as well, those who already participate in eternal life are invoked, whereas in the memento for the dead after the Consecration all those still in need of purification and prayer are remembered.

In other words, congregation stretches not only over the whole earth but also far beyond the borders of death. About those gathered around the altar, the horizons of time and space roll back, revealing as the real, sustaining community the whole of saved humanity.

This congregation in toto then is the Church, sustainer of the holy act of worship. That the Mass is something quite different from the private religious act of an individual is obvious, but it is also more than the divine service of a group of individuals united by like beliefs (that of a sect, for instance). It is the Church with all the breadth that the word implies, the universal Church. We begin to visualize her scope when we read what Saints Paul and John write of her. There, even her ultimate earthly limits dissolve to make her one with all saved creation. Her attributes are "the new man," "the new heaven," and "the new earth!" (Eph. 2:16; 4:24; Rev. 21:1).

Nor is the Church merely the sum total of the saved plus the totality of things; rather, it is a living unit, an organism formed and composed around a reigning, all-permeating figure: the spiritual Christ. She has full powers to proclaim Christ's teaching and bestow His sacraments; respect or disrespect to her involves God Himself. What sustains the Mass is not only an endless legion of hearts and spirits, the faith and love of all creation, but also a supernatural society endowed with authority and bearing responsibilities.

Our task is to find our place in the enormous whole. This is not easy. Man has a tendency to spiritual intimacy and exclusiveness, which causes him to shrink from such magnitude and grandeur. There is also the resistance of modern religious feeling to the visible Church in its realistic sense: resistance to office and order, to authority and constitutionality. We are all too subjective, inclined to count as truly religious only the direct and spontaneous experience. Order and authority leave us cold. Here self-discipline is especially necessary. The text of the Mass repeatedly reveals the attitude that has been called Roman, an attitude that rests precisely upon the consciousness of formal institutional unity, God-given authority, law and order. This may strike us as strange, perhaps even as unreligious—we spoke of this before in our discussion of the Collects. Those same Collects express something very important for us. Not only are we as Christians "congregation," not only "saved mankind" and "new creation"; we ourselves are "Church," so we must consent to and patiently educate ourselves in this given role.

18

Habit as a Hindrance

What actually hinders us from taking part in the Mass as we should? First of all, habit.

It is a fundamental spiritual law that every impression exhausts itself. All life is a perpetual becoming, but also a perpetual perishing. Thus an impression starts out strong, gains in strength, lasts for a while, then fades. He who has experienced it has used it up, and indifference sets in.

This is as it should be as long as it is a question of the many fleeting contacts of daily life; each has its moment or moments and then makes way for the next. But the same process becomes fatal when permitted to govern relations that are a fundamental part of our existence and consequently irreplaceable: our vocation, for instance, with its unchanging demands and responsibilities; marriage; genuine friendship; or our relations to self, since we are as we are and must find some sort of *modus vivendi* with ourselves. Here the law of diminishing impressions and emotions can cause serious difficulties. When a task is new and full of interest, it seems to perform itself. When it has been performed for a long time it becomes burdensome and difficult. The company of another person is joyful and stimulating as long as yet unknown responses in his thinking or surprises in his attitude refresh us; but after closer acquaintance, when we begin to know beforehand exactly how we will react and reply, boredom sets in. As for ourselves, we all have experienced discouragement with our shortcomings and oppressive disgust with our own nature.

All this applies to Holy Mass as well. We hear it every Sunday; many people hear it more often, even daily. It is always pretty much the same, most of the principal texts recurring time and again. Even the variable parts of the Mass resemble one another in construction, language, and spiritual attitude. The Graduals, for example, are usually patterned after the biblical proverbs and interspersed with alleluias. The Collect always begins with the direct address, then develops the principal thought, and finishes off with the formal end clause. In time, even the changing Epistle and Gospel readings lose their freshness. After years of following the sacred ceremony, we begin to respond to it as to an old, familiar friend.

Thus at first fleetingly, then ever more prolonged and powerfully, the feeling of monotony creeps in: "I know

all that. I know exactly what words follow every move."
When in addition the same priest appears at the same altar over a long period, officiating in the same manner with
his unchanging personal peculiarities and shortcomings,
a veritable crisis of boredom and weariness can overcome
us. We no longer "get anything out of it," hardly know
why we still go. The fact that Church law requires Sunday attendance sometimes only adds to our difficulties.

What shall we do—stay away? When the Mass threatens to become a habit for someone who goes regularly
during the week, it is certainly advisable for him to attend
less frequently, perhaps only on Sundays for a while, sub-
stituting visits in the quiet church or Bible reading. But
this remedy is not possible for the Sunday churchgoer,
whose attendance is required on that day. It is claimed
that religious life must come from within and should not
be forced, yet man lives not only spontaneously but also
in the practice and discipline of an ordered existence.
Whenever he abandons these, something valuable is lost.
The rule about Sunday attendance is therefore not only
necessary but right, the more so as it applies to sacred
time, the day of the Lord and its relation to the rest of
the week. But behind the pedagogical standpoint is another and more important consideration: the fact that
Christ instituted the mystery of the Mass, so that it is not

something we can ignore at whim, but the essential core of our religious life. And if we really were to omit it, what should we put in its place? We would devise something of our own choosing and soon experience a much worse satiety: the insupportable triviality of human endeavor where the ultimate meaning of existence is at stake.

Then what can we do? First, make it clear to ourselves once and for all that Holy Mass belongs in our lives. In the conviction of a thing's finality and inalterability lies a peculiar strength. As soon as I am convinced that I should perform some act, I can do it—at least up to a certain point. Anything but steadfast by nature, man is always ready to let things slide; this definite law in his life is something like the bones in his body, giving him firmness and character.

"Sing ye to the Lord a new canticle" (Ps. 96 [95]:1, Douay-Rheims). This singing should soar fresh from the heart renewed. Man is capable of breaking through the monotony of long-continued doing and seeing and, by inner readiness, of beginning anew.

This is particularly true of Holy Mass, which is something absolute and inexhaustible. Its central reality is the saving act of the living Christ, which contains the fullness of God's wisdom and love, not merely as objects received, but as vital and operative forces. At the celebration of the Lord's memorial we are not dependent on our own faculties of perceiving and appreciating; Christ works with us. Primarily it is He who acts; in our "remembering," it is Christ Himself who stirs.

Faith tells us that monotony cannot come from what the Mass itself is; it can make its appearance, but only in us, when we do not take Christ and His love seriously enough. Christ is new precisely to the extent that the believer occupies himself with Him. Every act of obedience, every self-conquest, every situation in life that we master through the Lord's direction and strength reveals something new in Him. The Mass gives as much as we ask of it. And the power of renewal is not limited to our own capacity for renewal; we can count upon God's infinite possibilities.

19

Sentimentality as a Hindrance

Sentimentality is essentially the desire to be moved: by loneliness or delight, by sorrow or dread; by greatness and exaltedness or by weakness and helplessness — somehow to be moved.

The need is greater with one person than with another, but we all have it to some extent. The sentimental believer's attitude toward the great figures of sanctity, the truths he prefers, the passages he frequently quotes, his whole bearing — everything disposes him to emotionalism.

Up to a certain point there is little that can be said against this; it is simply a predisposition, like a fuzzy mind or weak muscles. But when a believer allows such a tendency to dominate him, it becomes disastrous, robbing revelation of its greatness, distorting the saints, and generally rendering his religious life soft, weak, unnatural, and embarrassing.

Examples of sentimentality meet us everywhere; we've only to glance at the popular spiritual-exercise leaflets, the average samples of religious art, or to read some of the meditations on Christ's passion or on the poor souls in Purgatory.

Much more could be said on the subject. At any rate, sentimentality is a force that must be reckoned with.

For the sentimental believer, participation in the Mass is extremely difficult. He finds the sacred act neither comforting nor edifying, but austere, coldly impersonal, almost forbidding. And for people like himself he is right. The Mass is austere. Its tremendous concepts are expressed tersely. Its action is simple. Its words are clear and concise; its emotion controlled. Its spiritual attitude is that of profoundest surrender, but still and chaste.

Sentimentality tries to gild the lily by transferring its own trimmings to the Mass. The altar, never meant to depart far from the pure form of the sacred table, becomes a pompous welter of cherubs and little lamps and much glitter; the action is garlanded with gestures contrived above all to touch the emotions; the servers' apparel is fussy and doll-like. Texts and music are of an ingratiating sweetness. In place of the missal's powerful language, we find Mass devotions abounding in artificial conceptions and soft, unnatural sentiments. Thus the central truth of the Mass is lost. The Lord's memorial becomes an "edifying" exhibition, and earnest participation in the sacred ceremony is supplanted by a touching experience.

The event which took place at the Last Supper in Jerusalem and the death which the Lord died on the Cross—both mysteriously interwoven, as His own words reveal—are renewed again and again. Christ commanded: "As often as ye shall do these things, ye shall do them in remembrance of me." The Church accepted the command, obeying it through the centuries to the end of time. How does she "do them"? In the strict form of the Liturgy.

The texts of the missal are clear and concise. Their tone is that of profound emotion, dignified and controlled. Jesus Himself is hardly addressed. Not at all during the Canon; briefly after the completion of the act of commemoration—in the Agnus Dei and in the prayers before Communion—always with great reserve. As a rule, the words of the Mass are addressed to the Father. There is no mention at all of the Lord's feelings during His Passion and dying. Veiled in deepest reverence, they stand mute behind the whole mystery.

As for the sacred action, here is neither mimicry nor sentimental, vicarious experience. What took place on Golgotha does not come to the fore at all, but remains eloquently silent behind the whole. The action is taken from the event in the Supper chamber, again not imitated but translated into a strict, stylized form that conceals as much as it reveals.

The early Christians believed that it was proper to clothe the sacred in mystery. One reason for their attitude was the danger of persecution, which profaned it at every opportunity; but they also knew that mystery is the natural element of holiness. This element has been lost to us, or allowed to sink into the twilight of emotionalism and false mysticism. Possibly one of the most pressing tasks of the religious renewal is to rediscover genuine mystery and the attitude it requires, an attitude that has nothing sentimental about it and that flatly refuses to facilitate the demands of faith, preferring to guard its full austerity and dignity. In the Liturgy alone may the only genuine arcane discipline still in existence be found and acquired.

The strict form of the Mass, therefore, aims at the exact opposite of what sentimentality desires. Sentimentality, which is desirous of being moved, employs to this end stirring gestures evocative of terror and helplessness, words dripping with feeling, exciting imagery, moving dialogue, and the like. Nothing of all this is to be found in the Mass; thus the sentimental believer has three choices: he can relinquish all hope of establishing vital contact with the Mass and retire into his own sphere of private devotions; he can falsify its character, turning it into a kind of moving Passion Play; or he can courageously face his inclinations and bring them to heel.

Sentimentality must be overcome; otherwise genuine contact with the Mass is impossible. The individual must discard once and forever the habit of judging it from his personal leanings and tastes, for its form is that which obedience to the Lord's command has received from His Church. Of course, here too exaggeration must be avoided. Neither her ceremonies nor their wording should assume the absoluteness of dogmas.

But this much is certain: the manner in which the Lord's memorial is executed in the Church is the *lex orandi*, the norm of divine service. He who really wishes to believe—in other words, to obey revelation—must obey also in this, schooling his private sentiments on that norm. Then it will be clear to him that here is at work a spiritual life of quite different dimensions from that of his personal piety. He will come to know feeling that emerges from the profundity of God. He will enter the inner realm of Christ. He will experience in himself the powers that govern the inner life of the Church.

20

Human Nature as a Hindrance

How exactly did the Lord institute the Eucharist? Considering what was happening, considering who was placing the essence of His being and work into an act which henceforth, constantly renewed, was to form the center of religious existence, one would suppose that He minutely determined everything—the structure of the whole as well as the details of words and action; that He protected this holy of holies from the disturbing and distorting effects of history by placing it in a spiritual preserve guarded by strict laws. The more so since the Old Testament tradition from which He came had developed elaborate religious rites, so that on the one hand He would find such specification only natural, and on the other He would consider it necessary in order to keep the line between the old and the new clear and definite.

Yet actually it was quite different. The Gospel reports show that Christ was completely filled with the significance of the moment. It is unthinkable that He could have been careless of anything. He does precisely what He set out to do. But what is that? In connection with the Passover feast, He takes bread, pronounces over it the words we know, and then offers it to His followers to eat. He does the same with the chalice. He says: "As often as ye shall do these things, ye shall do them in remembrance of me."

It is plain whom He means: the Apostles and their successors. What they must do is also evident: these things that He Himself has just done, without warping or spiritualizing them. That is all. Nothing more is said: no instructions on how the act is to be worked out in detail, its position in a greater whole or frame, when and where it is to be performed, and all the other questions that naturally arise. Thus the terse command of infinite possibilities and divine dignity is laid with startling simplicity in human hands.

Jesus drew upon the situation of the Passover for the sacred act and commanded that in future it continue to be celebrated in this new form. In brief, He arranged no proceedings; He planted a seed, which promptly took root in the young congregation and unfolded there. The Church has always known that what took place on Holy Thursday was to be renewed in the celebration of the

Eucharist: not in the form of mimicry, but as a vital realization. The seed has always been directly affected by its soil—by all the forces, motives, circumstances that affected its growth, again by the size of the congregation, by its urban or rural location, by the kind of people in it and the historical and cultural situation in which they found themselves.

Thus the cornerstone of the sacred act was laid in history—and what long and diversified history! There could not fail to appear, along with its vital, indestructible aspects, others bound to prove transitory, soon to become extinct. The whole structure had to settle sometime in the process, shifting certain concepts out of line. Sometimes less valuable additions managed to creep into language or ritual, and there were other dangers, quite aside from the hazards of the "dead language" employed.

Another thing: Holy Mass is celebrated by people, by a priest and servers and the congregation. All are human. One is deeply appreciative of the special nature and form of the Liturgy; another is not. One responds easily to symbols; another only to ideas or moral precepts. Even within a single individual the degrees of readiness and spiritual participation fluctuate. There are alert and joyous periods, but also periods of indifference and despondency, carelessness and dullness.

Human Nature as a Hindrance

God's sacred act is planted in human imperfection. Celebrated by a priest for whom the Liturgy is really alive, its words and gestures are convincing; by one who is not immersed in the spirit of the Liturgy, they are apt to appear forced and unnatural. Then there are all the private little shortcomings of speech and bearing and movement that can be so distracting. The same is true of the congregation. It too can be understanding or indifferent, can actively participate or merely allow events to take their course. It can be educated to the celebration of the Mass and really understand; but it can also passively watch the ceremony unwind, an accepted tradition, day after day, Sunday after Sunday. It can enter into the sacred action or remain outside, carrying on its private devotion with all the varying shades of mood that ever-variable human life contains.

For the individual believer this can present serious difficulties. When he goes to Holy Mass he finds it as it is with all its inadequacies. Everything depends on whether he remains a spectator who expects to be "offered something decent"—and is accordingly pleased or disappointed—or whether he understands that it is a question of service performed together, hence depending not only on the priest and the rest of the congregation, but also on himself.

Everyone is responsible for the celebration of the Mass, each according to his qualifications. As far as he is able to act within the established order, the individual should do everything in his power to perfect a practice or remove an abuse. Beyond that, he must accept the Mass he attends as it happens to be. He must not be unduly upset by its limitations; certainly he must not use them as an excuse to withhold his share of participation. He should remind himself that the essential remains untouched and should enter into it and help to accomplish the sacred act.

21

The Mass as Institution

Holy Mass is the heart of the direct relationship between God and believer. When the Christian goes to church, he leaves the world of ordinary human existence behind and steps into the hallowed spot set apart for God. There he remains with the others of the congregation, a living offerer of the sacred service celebrated before God's countenance.

What we do in this area reserved for God does not spring directly from our religious experience or desire; neither do we all gather in church to express to God our pressing wants as though in response to a great general need. This too is possible and natural, and it belongs to the most powerful religious experiences that a man can have: the united appearance before Him from whom everything comes and to whom everything returns.

What happens in Holy Mass, however, is different. The Mass is not the immediate expression of an existence capable of understanding and redeeming itself spiritually. It is not a creation of that power which shaped the word of praise and the revelatory act from the emotion of the hour, but something long since independently arranged, ordered, and declared valid once and forever. It does not arise each time from the individual's or the congregation's relation to God, but descends from God to the believer, demanding that he acknowledge it, entrust himself to it, and do it. It owes its existence not to Christian creativeness, but to Christ's institution.

Consequently, the Mass cannot be celebrated by anyone, but only by one who is authorized. When the father is still the recognized head of the family (also its spiritual head), he can institute a custom or a celebration that becomes binding for the family. Likewise the bearer of a religious office, the priest, or (if he has spiritual authority) the king can institute a religious celebration for a certain diocese or kingdom. Religious history has countless illustrations of this.

But the institution that concerns us here is not only valid for a family or a race or an empire, but claims to be the absolute norm of religious celebration, the heart of spiritual life for all peoples and for all ages. No human being has the power to set up such a statute. No earthly authority having such absolute power could exist, not even with the reservation that all genuine power comes from God.

God never empowered any human being to institute an act obligatory for all peoples and ages. This does not mean that He could not have done so, but simply that He did not.

He who did establish the unique universal institution of the Mass was no mere messenger of God, no prophet, high priest, or king, but the Son of the eternal Father, God incarnate in history, who could say of Himself: "All power in heaven and on earth has been given to me" (Matt. 28:18). It is He who proclaims the saving truth to all men and to all ages: not as the prophets proclaimed it, "Thus speaketh the Lord," but, "I say to you" (see Matt. 5:21-28). He does not even say: "My Father speaks to you through me," but: "I myself say ..." And He adds: "Heaven and earth will pass away, but my words will not pass away" (Matt. 24:35). "Go into the world and preach the gospel to every creature. He who believes and is baptized shall be saved, but he who does not believe shall be condemned" (Mark 16:15-16). At the close of the Sermon on the Mount Jesus declares that obedience to His words is the sole basis on which life capable of existing in eternity can be founded; all life founded on anything else will disintegrate under God's gaze.

Not for nothing was the name reserved solely for God applied immediately to the Son: *Kyrios Christos*. It appeared with the ease of a foregone conclusion, of necessity, since He actually was the Lord, whose sovereignty covers not only material reality but also that which is immeasurably greater: the law and the covenant. When the Pharisees protest that Jesus' disciples are breaking the law by plucking ears of grain on the Sabbath, He replies: "The Son of Man is Lord even of the Sabbath" (Matt. 12:8), and with the Sabbath, the entire law. At the Last Supper He formally declares the old covenant fulfilled and He proceeds to establish the new heart and mainspring of religious life, the Eucharist (cf. Luke 22:20).

We know exactly when and how He went about it. The Gospels of Matthew, Mark, and Luke describe how Jesus, before His death, celebrated the Passover for the last time with His disciples. During that feast, whose celebration differed sharply from the traditional form, He instituted the new feast in His memory and the new covenant in His blood. St. John reports the speech Jesus made at Capernaum, where He promised men His Eucharistic flesh and blood (cf. John 6). Finally, St. Paul speaks of it in the eleventh chapter of his first letter to the Corinthians, where he stresses the fact that the Lord Himself revealed it to him (1 Cor. 11:23).

God ratified what Jesus instituted. Man has here no call to create or determine; his task is to obey and act. Moreover, the institution itself is entrusted to a special authority for protection and guidance.

It is conceivable that the Lord could have instituted the mystery and then left it to the pious inspiration of the believers. Had He done so, it would have passed through history, formed and colored by the peculiarities of various governments, races, epochs. The development of its central theme would have been handed over to the experience and creative powers of the believers. But this is not what Christ did. He did not entrust His institution to the freely streaming spirit or to the religious inspiration of the moment, but to an office that He Himself established. He wanted His followers to live not as a loose collection of individuals with their sundry convictions and experiences, but as a constitutional unit, as a Church. When He chose the Apostles He was already conferring office and authority upon the Church: "Amen, I say to you, whatever you bind on earth shall be bound also in heaven; and whatever you loose on earth shall be loosed also in heaven" (Matt. 18:18). "He who hears you, hears me; and he who rejects you, rejects me; and he who rejects me, rejects Him who sent me" (Luke 10:16). That office was to continue through history: "all days, even unto the consummation of the world" (Matt. 28:20). Consequently the Apostles were to have successors to whom that office could be passed.

To this office, to the Church, Christ's institution was entrusted. Her authority determines the form and details of the sacred service. Although it has adapted itself to the characteristics of peoples and periods during the course of centuries, its core has remained the same, and it is the Church that has kept it intact. The adaptations themselves sprang only partly from the differences of historical settings; the predominant cause for all modifications was the ecclesiastical office itself which, constantly active, adapted and rearranged details, yet preserved the efficacy and unity of the whole.

We begin to see the attitude that is required of us: faith, piety, and vital participation. These are not to be shaped and guided solely by private experience and religious creativeness, nor are they to be given free rein; they are to be practiced in the spirit of acceptance and obedience. When believers attend Holy Mass they go not to express their own religious emotion nor to receive direction and inspiration from the spiritual talents of a man who enjoys their special trust. They enter into an order established by God; they go to participate in a prescribed service.

22

The Memorial of the New Covenant

How did Jesus establish the act by which He passed on to His followers the memorial of His Person and of His redemptory fate? According to St. Luke, He did so as follows:

> The day of the Unleavened Bread came, on which the Passover had to be sacrificed. He sent Peter and John, saying, "Go and prepare for us the Passover that we may eat it."
>
> But they said, "Where dost Thou want us to prepare it?"
>
> And He said to them, "Behold, on your entering the city, there will meet you a man carrying a pitcher of water; follow him into the house into which he goes. And you shall say to the master of the house, 'The Master says to thee, "Where is the guest chamber, that I may eat the Passover there

with my disciples?" ' And he will show you a large upper room furnished; there make ready." And they went, and found just as He had told them; and they prepared the Passover.

And when the hour had come, He reclined at table, and the twelve Apostles with Him. And He said to them, "I have greatly desired to eat this Passover with you before I suffer; for I say to you that I will eat of it no more, until it has been fulfilled in the kingdom of God." And having taken a cup, He gave thanks and said, "Take this and share it among you; for I say to you I will not drink of the fruit of the vine, until the kingdom of God comes."

And having taken bread, He gave thanks and broke it, and gave it to them, saying, "This is my body, which is being given for you; do this in remembrance of me." In like manner He took also the cup after the supper, saying, "This cup is the new covenant in my blood, which shall be shed for you." (Luke 22:7-20)

It is the feast of the Passover, which in accordance with the law is celebrated annually before the great Easter Sabbath as a fulfillment of the divine command recorded in the twelfth chapter of the book of Exodus.

The Memorial of the New Covenant

For centuries the Hebrews had been living in slavery in Egypt. Then God ordered Moses to command Pharaoh to liberate them. Pharaoh had refused, and the mysterious plagues sent by God to overcome his resistance had affected him only briefly. Now the last and most dreadful of the plagues, designed to break his stubbornness, was at hand: the death of all the firstborn in the land, of men and of beasts. But to prove to His people that He was the Lord and to burn the memory of the liberation deep into their consciousness, God gave the event a form that could not fail to impress itself on the mind and the emotions alike. He commanded every Hebrew family to slaughter a lamb and to paint the doorposts with its blood, so that the angel of death on his way through the land would see the sign and pass over (Exod. 12:11-14). Not only was the memory of this event to be kept alive by record and recollection, it was to be celebrated each year in liturgical ceremony. Thus God instituted the feast of the Passover, or Pasch.

At first the celebration had the form of a grave memorial; but gradually it assumed the character of a joyous festival. The meal grew increasingly rich. Those at table no longer stood, girt for the journey and staff in hand, but reclined comfortably; no longer did they eat in the originally prescribed haste, they dined in untroubled leisure.

During the meal the host described the great event that was being commemorated in such a manner that those present could imagine themselves back in the days of Moses.

Jesus broke this pattern. He who knew Himself Lord of the law and the covenant put an end to the thought hitherto commemorated and established instead a new memorial. Similarly He put an end to the covenant that had been established by the event commemorated, and He sealed the new covenant of redemption with His death.

We can see the exact place where Jesus intervened. The cup mentioned by St. Luke in the foregoing passage is the third cup of the Pasch. One interpreter beautifully complements the Lord's words, "Take this and share it among you" with "for the last time according to ancient rite." Then Jesus takes bread, offers thanks, breaks it and gives it to them; again the act which the host had always performed, only now it receives a new significance in Jesus' accompanying words: "This is my body, which is being given for you." Whereupon He takes the cup, "after the supper," as the host had always taken it, blesses it, thanks God, and offers it—again with the new significance of His words: "This cup is the new covenant of my blood, which shall be shed for you."

The Memorial of the New Covenant

The old covenant, sealed with the blood of sacrificial animals, is at an end. Now a new covenant has been sealed, again with blood, that of Christ. He Himself is offered up, like the lamb they have just slaughtered and consumed: His body, "which is being given for you"; His blood, "which shall be shed for you."

Here, too, it is a commemoration: "Do this in remembrance of me." St. Paul continues the thought in his first letter to the Corinthians, in which he writes: "For as often as you shall eat this bread and drink this cup, you proclaim the death of the Lord, until He comes" (1 Cor. 11:26).

That is the event upon which the institution of the Mass rests. Christ Himself, His love, and His redeeming fate are its contents, which He poured into the mold of the ancient covenant, now brought to completion. Only the form remains, the ceremonial supper. Henceforth, the new covenant is there to contain those contents to the end of history, "until He comes."

23

Reality

At the Last Supper we saw how the Lord established institution upon institution: the memorial of His saving love and its covenant between God and the new holy people upon the memorial of the liberation from Egypt under the Old Covenant, now completed.

Those who believe in Him are to come together and "do this," to do exactly what He did on that last evening. The command involves Him too; for when His followers obey and do, what happened then will happen again, just as when He Himself acted. They are to take bread, give thanks, bless it, and speak over it the words He spoke. They are to take the chalice and again thank, bless, speak as He did.

Not just anyone is entitled to do this, but only those whom Jesus addressed at that time, His table companions at the last Passover, the Apostles, to whom He had already committed His authority (cf. Matt. 10); after them, those to whom they in turn would pass on their powers: the bishops and their assistants in the divine office, the priests.

When the priest performs what the Lord commanded, all act with him, so that after the Lord's death one can truly say that "they," the believers, "continued steadfastly in the teaching of the Apostles and in the communion of the breaking of the bread and in the prayers" (Acts 2:42). "And continuing daily with one accord in the temple, and breaking bread in their houses, they took their food with gladness and simplicity of heart, praising God and being in favor with all the people" (Acts 2:46-47).

From this we see that at that time the Christians were still living in the old order, observing the prescribed services of the Temple as the others did. They had not yet realized that the Temple with its services, together with the entire order of the Old Testament, was ended and that a new life pattern was slowly taking shape. Already the little community has something entirely of its own, the ceremonial breaking of bread "in their houses." In all probability, groups of early Christians met in homes large enough for the purpose.

At first there was simply an ordinary meal, an expression of fraternal unity, and a means of helping the poorer among them. Sometimes however (probably on

Sundays), the meal took on a special, festive note (cf. Acts 20:7). It was always a real meal, although judging from St. Paul's first letter to the Corinthians, it was not always an entirely spiritual affair! The letter is concerned chiefly with current abuses, but it also suggests how those gatherings were supposed to be, and how—at least in the beginning—they usually were.

Then, at a certain moment in the meal, the Lord's representative took bread and the cup, acting as the Lord had commanded him to do. Before this it has been a commemoration in the spirit only, a speaking and hearing, weighing and accepting: now it is still commemoration, but of a totally different kind. For that which was commemorated during the first part of the Mass was not actually present, save in the imagination of the believers, in the continually efficacious love and grace that stirred in their hearts and souls. Now the significance of the event changes. The moment the priest, as the Lord's representative, speaks the words "This is my body," what is "commemorated" is also actually present in truth and in reality.

"This is my body," "this is my blood"; under no circumstance may the *is* in these holiest of sentences be interpreted as "means" or "is a symbol of" "my body and blood." If ever the Lord's admonition, "Let your speech be, 'Yes, yes'; 'No, no'; and whatever is beyond these comes from the evil one" (Matt. 5:37) was deeply urgent, it is here.

It is not only wrong but sacrilegious to tamper with these words. What they express is simplest truth, and what takes place pure reality. He who speaks them is neither a great nor the greatest religious personality of millennia, but the Son of God.

His words are no expression of mystical profundity, but a command of Him who has all earthly and heavenly power. They have no equivalent in human speech, for they are words of Omnipotence. We can compare them only with other words of the Lord, when "He arose and rebuked the wind and the sea, and there came a great calm" (Matt. 8:26); or, to the leper: "I will, be thou made clean" (Matt. 8:3); or to Jairus's dead child, "Girl, arise!" (Luke 8:54). Their real equivalent is the Father's "Be!" from which creation itself emerged (Gen. 1:3).

Christ gave these sacred words to those He delegated to guard and to execute His memorial. Their origin does not lie in the priest or in the bishop who speaks them but in Christ, who gave them to priest and bishop. Yet because they are God-given through grace, they become the priest's own words when he speaks them in obedience to Christ. Hence the Mass is a commemoration, but it is a commemoration of a very special kind. By the words of the Transubstantiation, what took place on Holy Thursday, Christ's gift of self as nourishment for eternal life, takes place again—in a form which also outwardly resembles the Savior's act on that holy night.

There can be no question of symbolism here. The Apostles were no modern psychologists or symbolists, but men of antiquity, whose thinking was characteristically objective and realistic. They had not forgotten the great speech at Capernaum in which Jesus had insisted (for many to the point of intolerability) on the fact that He was to offer Himself as real food and real drink, thus forcing His followers to an uncompromising either-or of faith.

There is not a trace of symbolism in the Acts of the Apostles or in the first letter to the Corinthians, or in any of the earliest Christian writing on this sacred mystery. Without exception it is taken as revelation, which we cannot call into question, asking whether it be possible. It is a communication and a command of God, for whom all things are possible.

Our attitude can be neither that of testing nor of criticizing; it can only be that of belief, and belief implies obedience. As it is a question of mystery, we must acknowledge it solely because of God's word. As soon as we lose sight of this fact, everything is lost. That is why there is the call of warning and reminding just prior to the heart of the Mass, the Consecration: the call "*mysterium fidei*." Do not forget: we have here a mystery of the faith!

24

Time and Eternity I

We call a great work or deed imperishable, but this is true only as long as there are men who cherish and perpetuate it. We all have the feeling that a genuine imperishableness must exist somewhere, but this is only a vague intuition, a claim on existence, a hope of some mysterious realm in which all that has achieved validity is preserved forever.

The feeling becomes clearer and more tangible only when we relate that realm to God, who receives all that is valid into His eternity. But the uneasy question remains: Is what man considers valid really so, even before God?

How was it with the Son of Man? In one way the transient quality of Jesus' life seems particularly and painfully evident to us, for not only did that life come to an end, as does all human life, but its unutterably divine costliness was prematurely demolished by a will so evil and so destructive that we never cease to wonder at how this was possible. But there was something more about Jesus—beyond the fact that His life, with every step He took, penetrated ever more deeply into the already perfect, into the already immortal.

We act upon decisions of the spirit, which is immortal and hence already has something of eternity about it. The decision itself, however, begins and ends in time. With Jesus it was different. His will was not only spiritual but was permeated by the divine will of the eternal Son of God. Thus even His decisions had an underlying depth that reached from the gesture of His hand to the divine resolution. They were no longer temporal, but eternal. Jesus' acts began, unfolded, and ended in time, but both the resolve from which they sprang and the power by which they were sustained were eternal. In brief, everything the Lord did took place in time but came from eternity; and since eternity is unchangeable, everything He did was immortal.

This is a great and impenetrable mystery. Earthly things are buried in transitoriness, and for us eternity is still only a hope. We are unable to bridge the two. God alone makes this possible through what Scripture calls "the new creation": transfiguration (Gal. 6:15; 2 Cor. 5:17).

The temporal is not erased, but assumed into eternity, there to acquire a quality for which we now have no concept. One day, though, our whole thinking, now locked in earthly transitoriness, will receive that liberating quality, and we shall be given along with the "new heaven and the new earth" (Rev. 21:1) the new eye, which really sees, and "the mind of the Lord" (1 Cor. 2:16).

This mode of being and seeing was Jesus', with whom it came into existence. He brought it to us, and in such a way that we might share in it. He is the new, the beginning. As long as He lived on earth that beginning remained veiled, but it was already here. He had to bear earthly bondage and transitoriness through to the end, because He had become "like us in all things" (2 Cor. 5:21) in order to expiate our sins. It was not until the Resurrection that the new was able to break through.

After the mysterious forty days in which, disregarding the laws of nature, He appeared and disappeared at will, seeming to hesitate incomprehensibly between time and eternity, He returned to the Father and is now completely eternal. There was a heresy that attempted to free the Son of God from the taint of earthliness by teaching that He left His body and everything connected with it here below and returned to pure divinity. Unfortunately, this teaching destroys the essence of all that is Christian.

The Son of the eternal Father became man in divine earnestness, which means He became man irrevocably.

Hence He remains man in all eternity. To be a man means to have a body, not an idealized, general sort of body, but one's own specific body. This is what St. John means when he writes in his first letter, "I write of what was from the beginning, what we have heard, what we have seen with our eyes, what we have looked upon and our hands have handled: of the Word of Life. And the Life was made known and we have seen, and now testify and announce to you, the Life Eternal which was with the Father, and has appeared to us ... in order that you also may have fellowship with us, and that our fellowship may be with the Father, and with His Son Jesus Christ" (1 John 1:1-3).

The "Life" or "body" "our hands have handled" is not only the unpassive form, but also gesture, deed, sufferings, and destiny. Everything that happened to the Lord is evident in His resurrected body. Scripture bears staggering witness to this fact in John's report of its wounds, so corporal and deep that the incredulous Thomas was able to obey Christ's command and put his hand into His side (John 20:27). These wounds are the banners of Jesus' life and fate, eternally received into His most vital being.

In that life nothing could be lost, for nothing took place that did not come from the everlastingness of that will with which the Son carried out the Father's decree in a historical, temporary act. Christ's entire life belongs to eternity. Two images express its imperishableness. The first appears in the deacon Stephen's great testimonial speech before the Sanhedrin: "But he, being full of the Holy Spirit, looked up to heaven and saw the glory of God, and Jesus standing at the right hand of God; and he said, 'Behold, I see the heavens opened, and the Son of Man standing at the right hand of God'" (Acts 7:55-56). The other image appears in the letter to the Hebrews, in the powerful passage in which Jesus, the true High Priest, strides through the courtyards of time across the threshold of death into eternity's holy of holies, bearing the sacrificial blood-offering of the New Testament before the majesty of the Father (Heb. 4:14; 5:10).

25

Time and Eternity II

What does the commemoration with which Jesus entrusted His followers signify? We are not going to try to understand now the relation between God's eternal life and events in time. The attempt would only result in a confusion of both concepts. One day we shall be able to understand—when we have been endowed with "the new," with that comprehension of the resurrected life which is the gift of grace. Now we can but sense the mystery of redeemed existence, feeling our way toward it with lowered eyes.

In this world, God's decree is fulfilled in the succession of temporal events; but God Himself is eternal—He always was and always will be. God realizes Himself both in universal space and in specific space or locality; He exists, however, in the pure here and now.

He manifests Himself in the differentiation of forms, relationships, characteristics; yet He Himself is of an undivided Oneness. Hence every hour with its content brushes God's eternity; every place with its content touches divine omnipresence; every form and every characteristic finds itself again in His all-inclusive simplicity. And what is true of God is true also of Him who sits at the right hand of the Father, Christ. His earthly life has been assimilated into eternity, henceforth to be linked irrevocably to every earthly hour redeemed by His destiny. The Lord's earthly life is directly applicable to everyone He loves, to every place, and in every situation. Wherever a man believes in Christ, he finds himself in direct contact with Him—and not only with the Son of God, but with the God-man in all the abundance of His redemptory existence on earth. St. Paul says that in every believer an unfathomable mystery unfolds: Christ above who "sitteth at the right hand of God" (Col. 3:1) is simultaneously below and within that believer. In all the richness of its salutary destiny, Jesus' life—His childhood, maturity, suffering, dying, and Resurrection—unwinds anew in every Christian, thus forming his real and everlasting existence. "It is now no longer I that live, but Christ lives in me" (Gal. 2:20).

What happens in a general manner whenever a person believes in the Lord, whenever Christ's redemptive life becomes that person's existence, takes place in a special, specific form in the commemoration which Jesus Himself established. The instant Christ's representative speaks His words over the bread and wine, Christ steps from eternity into place and hour, to become vitally present with the fullness of His redemptory power in the form of the particular, created species of bread and wine. There is no approach to this sacred procedure from our earthly experience. We can say neither that it is possible nor that it is impossible. We can only accept it as God's mystery of faith, this truth that is the beginning of all beginning. It is the truth by which a man is summoned, which he obeys, to which he entrusts himself, and from which his thinking takes its new point of departure. Once given and accepted, this beginning becomes the key to infinite realms.

When the intellect attempts to pin down this truth in concepts or to express it in words, it becomes very difficult. But is it in itself so difficult? Words do not seem to hit the mark. Actually it is not difficult but mysterious, although it can become difficult—in the sense of the listeners at Capernaum, who rejected Jesus' revelation: "This is a hard saying. Who can listen to it?" (John 6:60). Such difficulty is a question of the heart's revolt against the new beginning, of the self-confinement of the world, shutting itself off from the true light (John

1:5-11). Once a person honestly desires understanding, he senses the truth without being able to express it. And again we turn to the example of Capernaum: "'This is why I have said to you, "No one can come to me unless he is enabled to do so by my Father."' From this time many of His disciples turned back and no longer went about with Him. Jesus therefore said to the Twelve, 'Do you also wish to go away?' Simon Peter therefore answered, 'Lord, to whom shall we go? Thou hast words of everlasting life, and we have come to believe and to know that thou art the Christ, the Son of God'" (John 6:68-70).

This is the rescuing act: we do not understand, but we believe. The words "mystery of faith" have a double significance. They warn: Beware of trying to judge with human values as your intellectual criteria! But they also invite: Believe your redeemed hearts, which feel the superabundance of the truth that saves!

26

Liturgical Form

Holy Mass commemorates the Person and redemptory destiny of Christ. The memorial of the Mass is celebrated not in the form of a play, but of a liturgy. The object commemorated is not imitated, but translated into symbols.

The procedure is divided into several parts. The first part of the Mass consists in readings from Scripture and prayers corresponding more or less to the psalms of praise and the host's account of the Exodus at the beginning of the Passover meal. Then in the Offertory the gifts of bread and wine are prepared. This is reminiscent of the disciples' preparations for the Last Supper described in Matthew (Matt. 26:17-19). Immediately after this, Jesus' institution itself is carried out: blessing, thanksgiving, and the sacred meal.

The original form has vanished. No longer is there a table around which the faithful gather. In its place stands the altar, and however close architectural arrangement has permitted it, it still remains essentially separated from the believer. At the altar stands the priest; opposite him, united as congregation, the believers. There are no bowls and pitchers, cups and plates on the altar—all these have been concentrated in paten and chalice. And even they are shaped to differentiate sharply from the customary instruments in daily use. The priest partakes of the sacred food and offers it to the believers in a manner entirely different from that of the ordinary meal. As for the food itself, its form has become so spiritualized that one can almost speak of the danger of its being unrecognizable as bread.

It is important really to understand this process of translation from one sphere of reality to another. It exists not only here. In man lives a soul, but the life of that soul is not of itself visible; it is unable to express itself alone. To do so, it must first become gesture, act, word; it must translate itself into the language of the body in order for us to grasp it. Herein lies the true essence of what the German calls *Leib*—the vital unit of heart, mind, and body, as distinguishable from the mere physique. *Leib* is not only a vessel or an instrument, but the visible manifestation of the soul.

In Jesus this relation between body and soul reappears in sublime form. When God's Son came to us, He did not reveal Himself directly as the Logos; He became man. Here in a man's human body lived divine reality, a reality which did not manifest itself in mysterious radiance or overwhelming power, but which was translated into the body, gesture, word, and act of the man Jesus. In that man God was heard and seen, as St. John so vividly expresses it: "And the Word was made flesh, and dwelt among us. And we saw His glory—glory as of the only-begotten of the Father—full of grace and truth" (John 1:14).

The Mass moves along much the same line. The event which took place in the room of the Last Supper was in the form of the Passover as it was then celebrated. Jesus sat at table, about Him the members of His "household," the disciples. He took a loaf of bread, broke it, and spoke over it certain words in the language He ordinarily used and in the voice usual to Him in particularly solemn moments. He handed the pieces to the guests, just as He had done earlier in the meal and during other Passover celebrations. He took the cup, also as usual, gave thanks, spoke the words of consecration, and handed it to the disciples. They ate and drank as they had always done. All this had the immediate form of daily reality, which it preserved for some time.

But gradually it assumes a different form, the liturgical. Now the action loses its directness and becomes

ceremonial and measured. At some points it only suggests; at others it elaborates on the essential, piously en-
closing and veiling it. The bread assumes a new, special
aspect; it becomes host. The cup becomes festive chalice;
the table, altar. In place of the presiding master we have
the delegated priest. The words spoken no longer spring
from the immediate feeling and inspiration of the officia-
tor, but are strictly prescribed.

Jesus' memorial had to assume this form if it was to remain a permanent part of the believers' Christian life. In
its imitative form it could have been celebrated only very
rarely; frequent repetition would have caused it to slip
into the bizarre and embarrassing. In its liturgical form it
can be celebrated at all times—on festive as on ordinary
days—and in all situations, whether of sorrow, joy, or
need. It has now become genuine daily service.

Of course, like any other characteristic form, the liturgical too has its dangers: it invites independent development according to its own laws. Then the ritualistic action
threatens to stifle the actual sacrifice, and the essential
can be discerned only with difficulty through a tangle of
forms. Moreover, the disparity between the liturgical and
the realistic forms may so far remove the principal event
from ordinary existence that it loses touch with everyday
life. Not infrequently these dangers have become reality;

for this reason, the business of liturgical work today is to do everything possible to present the original form in its full clarity and power.

The believer is faced with an important task: that of discerning the essential in what meets his eye. In the altar he must see the table; in the priest, the head of the congregation; in the Host, the bread; in the chalice, the cup. He must recognize the Eucharistic Supper in the sacred act with its strictly prescribed wording. It is not enough, however devoutly, to "keep up with" a mysterious celebration's prayers and hymns, readings, and acts of consecration and offering. The believer must also follow the "translation" into symbols of everything that is taking place. When we watch a person we love, we do not merely observe his expression and gestures; we try to interpret those external manifestations of what is going on within. Here we have something similar, only greater. Speaking for himself and for his fellow Apostles, St. John says: "I write of what was from the beginning, what we have heard, what we have seen with our eyes, what we have looked upon and our hands have handled: of the Word of Life. And the Life was made known and we have seen, and now testify and announce to you, the Life Eternal which was with the Father, and has appeared to us. What we have seen and have heard we announce to you, in order that you also may have fellowship with us, and that our fellowship may be with the Father, and with His Son Jesus Christ. And these things we write to you that you may rejoice, and our joy may be full" (1 John 1:1-4).

27

The Bread of Life

Two things are necessary for true understanding. The first is the ability to compare, differentiate, and discern causal relations and interdependencies. This is important, but more important is something unteachable, a certain sensibility to the essence of things.

The real prerequisite of enlightenment is an intellectual and more than intellectual readiness to be struck and shaken by the revelatory impact of a thing, but not because of any personal fear or desire (for here we are already beyond the range of intent and purpose) and not for the sake of diversion (for at this level things cease to belong to the interesting). Confronted with the hidden meaning behind some image or pattern of images, a man is moved to disclose it and to clear for it a path into the open, so that truth may come into its own.

In the realm of faith, sensibility to the essence of things also exists, although of course in a different way.

Here the birth of a truth, the emergence of its essence into the light and spaciousness of recognition, are made possible not by any contact of intellect with significance, but by the power of God's light: grace. The object does not step from the world to confront the mind capable of discovering it; it does not exist in itself at all (in the manner of earthly objects, which can be grasped, plumbed, exploited by exhaustive study); it exists only in God and must be given, revealed by the Divine Word, and received by faith. It always remains a mystery that transcends the created mind.

The Lord's memorial is the central mystery of our Christian life. It has taken the form of a meal at which He offers Himself as the food. We were taught this in the Communion instruction of our childhood; we hear it repeated again and again in sermons and retreats; we read it in religious books. Yet are we really aware of the stupendousness of the thought?

It must have been important to the Lord that His hearers were conscious of it, for when He proclaimed the establishment of the mystery He stressed the enormity of it in a manner that could not have been accidental. His words at Capernaum sound quite different from those of the actual establishment, where they are frugal and calm. During the tremendous act that took place on Holy Thursday

He no longer dwells on its tremendous significance. The great test of faith has already taken place; the decision has fallen, and those who hear Him now have already proven themselves. For at Capernaum Jesus so drastically confronted His hearers with the otherness of the divine that they were not only struck, but struck down. The report reads: "I am the bread of life. He who comes to me shall not hunger, and he who believes in me shall never thirst" (John 6:35). The Jews "murmured about Him because He had said, 'I am the bread that has come down from heaven.' And they kept saying, 'Is this not Jesus the son of Joseph, whose father and mother we know? How, then, does He say, "I have come down from heaven"?'" (John 6:41-42).

The protest is directed not at the mystery of the Eucharist, which has not yet been proclaimed, but at Jesus' claim to be, in person, the bread of faith, eternal truth. What does the Lord do? He does not mitigate what He has said; He does not attempt to explain by pointing out His place in the sacred prophecies.

He goes further, pressing the sharp point of the blade home: "I am the bread of life. Your fathers ate the manna in the desert, and have died. This is the bread that comes down from heaven, so that if anyone eat of it he will not die.... If anyone eat of this bread he shall live forever."

Now they feel the full shock of the blow: "and the bread that I will give is my flesh for the life of the world" (John 6:48-52).

It would seem to be high time to modify these words or at least to explain them. Instead of coming to the rescue of His floundering hearers Jesus adds: "Amen, amen, I say to you, unless you eat the flesh of the Son of Man, and drink His blood, you shall not have life in you. He who eats my flesh and drinks my blood has life everlasting, and I will raise him up on the last day. For my flesh is food indeed, and my blood is drink indeed. He who eats my flesh, and drinks my blood, abides in me and I in him" (John 6:53-57). At this the first split runs through the group of disciples: "Many of his disciples therefore said, 'This is a hard saying. Who can listen to it?'" (John 6:61-62).

Jesus' closest followers are hard-pressed, but He does not help them. He forces them to a decision of life or death: are they ready to accept the fullness of revelation, which necessarily overthrows earthly wisdom, or do they insist on judging revelation, delimiting its "possibilities" from their own perspective?

"Does this scandalize you? What then if you should see the Son of Man ascending where He was before? It is the spirit that gives life; the flesh profits nothing. The words that I have spoken to you are spirit and life. But there are some among you who do not believe" (John 6:62-65). "The Jews" who first "murmured" against Jesus have already dispersed. Now also "many of his disciples" leave Him. Jesus turns to the remaining hard core: "Do you also wish to go away?" (John 6:68-69).

Still not a word of help, only the hard, pure demand for a decision. Peter replies: "Lord, to whom shall we go? Thou hast words of everlasting life, and we have come to believe and to know that Thou art the Christ, the Son of God" (John 6:68-70). They do not understand either, but struck by the power of the mystery, they surrender themselves to it. They are dumbfounded but trustful — at least most of them.

Not all, as we see from Jesus' reply: "'Have I not chosen you, the Twelve? Yet one of you is a devil.' Now He was speaking of Judas Iscariot, the son of Simon; for he it was, though one of the Twelve, who was to betray Him" (John 6:70-71).

It was to such rigorously tested men that Jesus entrusted the mystery of the Holy Eucharist; it was they who at the Last Supper first received the sacred nourishment.

28

Christ's Offering of Self

Every believer worthy of the name must sometime undergo the danger of scandal and its trial by fire. Some, the intrinsically shielded children of God, are able to come through; certainly not the majority.

We, too, must have felt the enormity of what took place at Capernaum, of that which so incensed the Jews and so shocked many of the disciples that they declared Jesus' words intolerable and left Him. It was the shock that probably shattered Judas' faith, the other eleven saving themselves only by a blind leap of trust to the Master's feet.

The impact of the message of Capernaum by no means leaves an impression of idyllic and sentimental wonderment, as the average book of devotions suggests. It is an unheard-of challenge flung not only at the mind, but, as we see from the stark scene at Capernaum, at the heart as well. There stands Christ and declares that He desires to give Himself to us to become the content and power of our lives. How can one person give himself to another—not things that he possesses, or knowledge or experience or help or trust or respect or love or even community of life—but his body and his soul to be our food and drink? And He means it really, not spiritually.

The quotation on which the Symbolists base their theory—"It is the spirit that gives life; the flesh profits nothing" (John 6:63)—by no means indicates that Jesus' words over the bread and wine were intended to mean: "My spirit shall fill you; my strength shall strengthen you." He might have said this, but He did not. The whole point of the speech at Capernaum is its insistence on real flesh, real blood, real eating and drinking in the spirit, of course, but that means in the Holy Spirit.

The Lord was referring to sacrifice, yes, but not as the hearers' familiarity with Temple sacrifice would suggest; not in the general, impersonal sense of the Old Testament, but in the intimate mystery of faith. The glorious reality of Jesus' sacrifice compares with the disciples' dim conception of it much as the risen body of the Lord in the full power of the Holy Spirit compares with the body that stands before them.

Nothing helps but to warn ourselves: here is the steepest, highest pinnacle of our faith (or the narrowest, most precipitous pass through which it must labor to reach full, essential freedom). Experience has shown that those who water down reality here at the summit of Christianity continue to do so all the way down the line: in their conceptions of the Church, of the Incarnation, of Christ's divine Sonship, of the truth of the triune God.

The test of Capernaum is in truth faith's supreme test. The man who refuses to master his feelings when they stand between him and God is unfit for the kingdom of God. This is where the great conversion, the change of measuring rods takes place. Not until the earnestness of the decision has been felt and the danger of scandal faced and overcome does the miracle of this ultimate mystery unfold. Then, suddenly, as if self-understood, comes the blissful knowledge that love perfectly fulfilled can give not only all it has, but all it is: itself.

No earthly love is ever perfectly fulfilled. To love in the earthly sense really means to strive for the impossible. St. John hints at the otherness of divine love: not only does God love; He is love! He alone not only desires to love, but can love "to the end" (John 13:1).

Jesus desires that men receive and make their own the gift of His vital essence, strength, His very Person as fully and intimately as they receive and assimilate the strength and nourishment of bread and wine. He even adds that the person who is not so nourished cannot possess ultimate life.

No earthly gift of love, even if it were possible, could ever be the perfect gift that Jesus' self-offering is—utterly devoid of accompanying impurities and toxins. He is total purity, total power, total vitality, and more: the prerequisite of that immortal, ultimate life which alone is capable of existence before God throughout eternity. Jesus really means what He said at the Last Supper: "Thomas said to him, 'Lord, we do not know where Thou art going, and how can we know the way?' Jesus said to him, 'I am the way, and the truth, and the life'" (John 14:5-6).

29

Encounter and Feast

Spiritual language has its own idiom for the coming of Christ in the Mass, which it expresses with great simplicity. Everywhere we meet sentences such as these: "Christ is present in the Mass"; "in Communion the Lord gives Himself to the communicant"; "He lingers with him." Referring to the promised Eucharist, the Lord Himself uses the image of a coming, an encounter.

Along with His insistence on the real eating and drinking of the real food, we find such sentences as: "For the bread of God is that which comes down from heaven and gives life to the world"; "[N]ot that anyone has seen the Father except Him who is from God, He has seen the Father"; "I am the living bread that has come down from heaven. If anyone eat of this bread he shall live forever; and the bread that I will give is my flesh for the life of the world"; "As the living Father has sent me, and as I live because of the Father, so he who eats me, he also shall live because of me" (cf. John 6:33-57). The "meat indeed" and "drink indeed" offered by the hand of the Father is not a thing but a Person; not it but He, the supreme Person praised in all eternity. Hence the reverent believer is naturally inclined to feel that the words about eating and drinking somehow debase the sacred Person of Christ.

St. John is the Evangelist who had to wage an endless battle against the heresies which began to crop up even in his lifetime. That is why his wording of the truth in all fundamental passages is extremely sharp. In his prologue he does not state that God's Son became man; he uses the more forceful expression: "The Word was made flesh" (John 1:14). In reference to the Eucharist he does not use the statement employed by the Synoptics: "Take and eat, this is my body," but: "He who eats my flesh and drinks my blood has life everlasting.... For my flesh is food indeed, and my blood is drink indeed. He who eats my flesh and drinks my blood abides in me and I in him" (John 6:54-56). Here is the ultimate clarification to which a man must speak his clear, decisive "Yes!" or "No!"

It is at this point that a difficulty becomes apparent, a genuine difficulty quite different from the stubborn contrariness of "the Jews," of the "many disciples," or of Judas at Capernaum. For here we have the valid fear that the

Lord's self-offering could be dragged from the purity of His relation to us as a person to the level of a mere thing or object. A person, and least of all He, the Holy One and Lord, cannot simply be given and taken and had; a person is not something to be passed about here and there. A person is not passed about; he comes, enters into a vital you-me relationship, gives himself freely and personally.

This is the second concept inherent in the Mass. The first was the meal; the second is the encounter. Both are expressed time and again by Christ Himself as well as by the general spiritual phrases His words have inspired. The one image is sustained by words such as "the true bread," the "food and drink," the "flesh for the life of the world"; the other by "come down from heaven," "he who comes to me," and by the countless expressions of the Lord's being among us, with us, His inclining lovingly toward us, His dwelling in us and uniting Himself with us.

The Mass is the Lord's memorial. We have tried to understand the word as richly and profoundly as possible; now we must go a step further.

The memorial which the Lord bequeathed to us is not merely the memory of an event or the portrayal of a great figure; it is the fulfillment of our personal relation to Christ, of the believer to his Redeemer. In the Mass, Christ comes in all His personal reality, bearing His salutary destiny. He comes not just to anyone, but to His own. Here again St. John brings this mystery into particularly sharp focus. God's Son comes from heaven, from the Father, whom He alone knows. He lives from the Father's vitality; everything He has and is, He has and is through the Father. But this intimate bond of love does not stop there. The Father sends His Son to men in order that He may pass on to them the divine life He has received. "As the living Father has sent me, and as I live because of the Father, so he who eats me, he also shall live because of me" (John 6:57).

When He became man, Jesus bridged the gulf between heaven and earth, between the Father and us once and for all. Henceforth He is with us in the sense that He belongs to us, is on our side: "Emmanuel," the God-who-has-come.

Yet in the special manner of the mystery, the Lord spans that gulf anew every time His memorial is celebrated. First, in the readings of the day, we receive word of Him. Then the offerings are prepared, and there is a pause. Through the Consecration, He comes to us, the subject of an incomprehensibly dynamic memorial, and gives us His grace-abounding attention. In Communion, He approaches each of us individually and says: "Behold, I stand at the door and knock" (Rev. 3:20). Insofar as the "door" swings open in genuine faith and love, He enters and gives Himself to the believer for his own.

This might be the place to mention the general significance of the Lord's coming in the Liturgy. What are the Christian implications of the word *feast*? What is the feast of Easter, for instance? The reality that lies at its core is the unique manner in which the Lord's Resurrection is renewed—not as a mere repetition, but so that He actually steps anew from eternity into our time, our presence. And He comes in the plenitude of His whole redemptory life each time in the particular mystery of the day that the unrolling liturgical year is commemorating: the mystery of God's Incarnation, or His Epiphany, or His Passion, or His Resurrection and Ascension. He comes to us from the Father in the power of the Holy Spirit.

To wait for Him, to invite Him, to go to receive and honor and praise Him, to be with Him, drawn into the intimacy of Communion with Him—that is the Christian feast.

We begin to see how closely interwoven the concepts of the *feast* and the *encounter* are. They do not conflict, but mutually sustain each other. Each prevents the other from one-sidedness and falsehood. The concept of the coming, the encounter, guards the dignity of the person and protects the concept of the Supper from unseemliness and irreverence. It reminds us that Communion is not possession but exchange, like the reciprocal gaze of any genuine *we*. On the other hand, the concept of the Supper projects that of the encounter to the incomprehensible holy mystery of ultimate intimacy. Among human beings an encounter is always relative; it never completely embraces the other person. This last unbridgeable separation is the exigency of all created love. In Holy Communion the last vestige of distance is removed, and we are assured of an "arrival" that surpasses all created possibility, genuine union.

30

Truth and the Eucharist

The action of the Lord's memorial embraces several different but inseparable concepts. We have already discussed two: that of the meal and that of Christ's coming or our encounter with Him. Behind both concepts, giving them their sacred significance, stands the tremendous fact of the redemptory sacrifice.

And still we have not touched bottom. One more thought belongs here: revelation and the pious recognition of divine truth. What does community with another person mean? Above all, it demands genuine mutual exchange, respect for his person, trust, loyalty, that simultaneous unity and reverence known as friendship or comradeship or love. Such an alliance surpasses the merely physical or merely spiritual. Because it rests on the will, it is capable of surviving the adversities to which all living things are exposed. But community has yet another element: the sharing of one another's power, radiance, vital depths; the ability to experience with the immediacy of sympathy and love the life of the other. These elements of community are essential and irreplaceable, but alone they still do not suffice. The relationship founded on them alone would have a blind spot. Between myself and the other there must be also truth. His essence must be conveyed to me. I must appreciate his uniqueness, his attitude toward life, his work and destiny. I must consent to his being as he is and make room for him, as he is, in my life. And I must know myself confirmed and accepted by him. Then our relations will be complete — not before.

The whole point of the Lord's memorial is such communion. No more complete communion exists than that which Christ established between Himself and those who believe in Him. Christ is not only "the Life"; He is also "the Truth." He is the incarnate Logos, God's Message written in flesh and blood. His self-offering is revelation; to receive Him is to receive Truth.

Once again we must consult the "commentary" to the institution of the Eucharist: Jesus' speech at Capernaum. The crowds have experienced the miracle of the loaves, and they press about Him expectantly. Now, surely, the miraculous bounty of the Messianic kingdom will be poured out! Jesus says to them: "Amen, amen, I say to you, you seek me, not because you have seen signs [that reveal divine truth], but because you have eaten of the loaves and have been filled. Do not labor for the food that perishes, but for that which endures unto life everlasting, which the Son of Man will give you" (John 6:26-27).

The people do not understand, so Jesus explains Himself more clearly: "'My Father gives you the true bread from heaven. For the bread of God is that which comes down from heaven and gives life to the world.' They said therefore to Him, 'Lord, give us always this bread.' But Jesus said to them, 'I am the bread of life. He who comes to me shall not hunger, and he who believes in me shall never thirst'" (John 6:32-35).

The life He speaks of is His own. The bread by which it is nourished is Himself. But how is that bread to be given and received? "All that the Father gives to me shall come to me, and him who comes to me I will not cast out" (John 6:37). In other words, it will be given through living contact with Him who is the Truth: on the one hand through the radiance of all He is and says and does and suffers; on the other, through our coming to Him and believing and seeing. What does one see? The divine figure of the Lord, in which the abundance of the invisible world breaks through. St. John says: "The Word was made flesh, and dwelt among us. And we saw His glory—glory as of the only-begotten of the Father—full of grace and truth" (John 1:14). What is to take place, then, is the revelation of Truth through God and the acceptance of that sacred truth by men.

Then the concept shifts. Again He says, "I am the bread of life." But He adds, "I am the living bread that has come down from heaven. If anyone eat of this bread he shall live forever; and the bread that I will give is my flesh for the life of the world" (John 6:51-52). This is so novel and unheard of that scandal sets in. Hasn't He Himself insisted again and again that "the bread" is His living flesh, that the eating is a true eating? Only the manner of that eating and drinking (namely, in the spirit) remains mysteriously veiled. "It is the spirit that gives life; the flesh profits nothing" (John 6:63). Christ has given His hearers the clue, but they refuse it.

The coherence of the speech as a whole is immeasurably important. Christ's memorial is an act of genuine sharing in His vital existence; it is not meant to be "spiritualized" or volatilized, for it is genuine eating and drinking, although in all the dignity, breadth, power, and significance of truth.

To participate in Holy Mass means to recognize Christ as the Logos, Creator, Redeemer. "As often as ye shall do these things, ye shall do them in remembrance of me." *Remembrance* here does not mean only: "Do this to commemorate me." It means in addition: "While doing this, think of me, of my essence, my tidings, my destiny; all these are the Truth." It is not by accident that the essential action of the Mass is preceded by the Epistle and Gospel, for each of the sacred texts is a clue to Christ's identity, is some facet of His personality or truth, some event in His life that comes forward to be understood and accepted. Each is a ray of that Truth which will be present at the Consecration no longer in word but in His real existence.

It is of primary importance that we see truth's relation to the Mass. Piety is inclined to neglect truth. Not that it shuns it or shies away from it, but it is remarkable how readily piety slides off into fantasy, sentimentality, and exaggeration. Legends and devotional books offer only too frequent and devastating proof of this; unfortunately piety is inclined to lose itself in the subjective, to become musty, turgid, unspiritual. Divine reality is never any of these, never falsely spiritual in the sense of the vaporous, the insubstantial. Divine reality, which is another name for truth, remains as divinely substantial as the living Jesus who walked the earth. But it must be illuminated by the spirit, the Holy Spirit.

Truth is essential to the fullness of the Mass. It is not enough to harp on the fact that the Mass is the center and content of the Christian's life. It must also be made clear how that center may be reached and that content shared. This is possible only when truth's vital relation to the Eucharist is recognized and when truth permeates the entire act of the sacred celebration.

31

The Mass and the
New Covenant I

Among the words Jesus used to establish His memorial, there is one which as a rule receives little notice in instruction on the Mass: the word about the covenant. The Gospel of St. Matthew reads: "All of you drink of this; for this is the blood of the new covenant, which is being shed for many unto the forgiveness of sins" (Matt. 26:28-19). St. Mark's: "This is my blood of the new covenant, which is being shed for many" (Mark 14:24). St. Luke's: "This cup is the new covenant in my blood, which shall be shed for you" (Luke 22:20). In St. Paul's first letter to the Corinthians, we also find a reference to the covenant, resembling that in Luke (1 Cor. 11:25).

We see how important the idea of the covenant is to the Church in the emphasis she places on it. At the Consecration of the wine in the Canon of the Mass we have the words: "For this is the chalice of my blood, of the new and eternal testament: the mystery of faith: which shall be shed for you and for many unto the remission of sins." What exactly does this mean?

The Passover was a feast of commemoration. Jesus Himself had celebrated the Passover each year with His disciples. But He had given the celebration a different turn by emphasizing not so much the liberation as the event following it: the sealing of the covenant of Sinai. The book of Exodus reports:

> And Moses wrote all the words of the Lord: and rising in the morning he built an altar at the foot of the mount, and twelve titles according to the twelve tribes of Israel. And he sent young men of the children of Israel: and they offered holocausts, and sacrificed pacific victims of calves to the Lord. Then Moses took half of the blood, and put it into bowls: and the rest he poured upon the altar. And taking the book of the covenant, he read it in the hearing of the people: and they said: All things that the Lord hath spoken we shall do. We will be obedient. And he took the blood and sprinkled it upon the people, and he said: This is the blood of the covenant which the Lord hath made with you concerning all these words. (Exod. 24:4-8)

The parallel is obvious. The mediator on Sinai says: "This is the blood of the covenant which the Lord hath made with you." Jesus says: "This is the chalice of my blood, of the new and eternal testament ... which shall be shed for you."

Behind the covenant of Sinai stands an earlier covenant, the one that existed between God and Abraham. It too had been sealed in blood. After the sun had set and a dark mist had risen, a lamplike fire passed between the "divisions" [of the slaughtered, sacrificial animals]. "That day God made a covenant with Abraham, saying: To thy seed will I give this land, from the river of Egypt even to the great river Euphrates" (Gen. 15:18). Still further back, in the gray beginnings of time, looms the original covenant between God and Noah, which was sealed after the Flood, when Noah offered his sacrifice to the Lord, who said, "I will no more curse the earth for the sake of man: for the imagination and thought of man's heart are prone to evil from his youth: therefore I will no more destroy every living soul as I have done." (Gen. 8:21). "Behold, I will establish my covenant with you, and with your seed after you.... And God said: This is the sign of the covenant which I give between me and you, and to every living soul that is with you, for perpetual generations. I will set my bow in the clouds, and it shall be the sign of a covenant between me, and between the earth" (Gen. 9:9-13).

In all these texts we find the reference to blood, often stressed again and again. This may impress us as strange, inhuman, but we do well to refrain from judging hastily. Deep in the consciousness of all races lies a knowledge of the power of blood. Blood is life in its primary and most elementary form. The flow of sacrificial blood diminishes tension, appeases anger, averts the lowering fate, enables life to reassume its course. How, it is impossible to say; we can only sense the truth of this. Somehow, through the flowing of blood a new beginning is made, mysteriously fortified by the sanguinary life-power. Obviously, the primitive significance of blood cannot simply be applied as it stands to revelation, for if ever anything needed re-demption, it is the dark, primeval powers of blood. How-ever, once existence has been transfigured, all things are revealed anew, and with them the power of blood.

It is significant in the covenant not because it is symbolic of the glory and terror of life, but because in a special way it belongs to God, the Lord of all life. The flowing of the sacrificial blood in the Old Testament is an acknowledgment of His sovereignty, signifying the opposite of what it signifies in other religious sacrifices. It is not a kind of blood-mysticism, not a release of the divinity in nature, not a summoning of the powers of the deep. It has nothing to do with any of these. It is simply the recognition and prayerful acknowledgment that God alone is Lord!

32

The Mass and the
New Covenant II

Upon the conception of streaming blood as an expression of ultimate obedience, God places His covenant. Again we must be careful to differentiate. The word does not signify here what it does in the various religions: the alliance of a divinity with a particular tribe. There it constitutes the secret vitality of the tribe, which in turn is the immediate expression of the god's reality. Thus the two are interdependent to the point of being or nonbeing: the tribe enjoys the power and protection of its god; on the other hand, the god lives from the fertility and strength of the tribe. Their unity is effected in sacrifice. Through his offerings man strengthens the vitality of his god; then, by consuming the offerings, man avails himself of his god's strength.

In the Old Testament there is not a trace of any such conception. God is not the divinity of a people or tribe because of any natural circumstance. He is not the mysterious source of its vitality and strength, but One who summons it from the freedom of divine decree. Certainly not because He needs human expression of His existence and a steady stream of earthly vitality in order to exist. He needs neither the Hebrew people nor any other people, for He is Lord of all that is. He summons this particular race not because it is better or more pious or more loyal than another. On the contrary, over and over again it proves itself disobedient, hardhearted, and inconstant.

What God founded with the Hebrew people was neither a powerful theocracy nor a religion expressive of a particular racial existence. He simply entrusted the Hebrews with His word and His law, which they were to bear through history, ultimately to all the peoples of the earth. Why He selected the Hebrews for this task is the impenetrable mystery of His decree.

All this must be clear if the word *covenant* is to receive its full weight. Above all, it is no question of a natural give-and-take, no alliance between the divine essence and the tribal, no blending of divine power with earthly, no beginning of a history of God in the history of a race. Not until all these conceptions have been cleared away does the inconceivable reveal itself: in absolute freedom the Lord of the universe singles out a people, addresses it and enables it to respond; He gives it His loyalty and demands its loyalty in return. He undertakes a divine task on earth and commands a race to render its services. If that race renounces its natural-historical existence in obedience to God's command, it will receive its fulfillment direct from divine sovereignty.

But the Hebrew people declined. They clung fast to their racial consciousness and will and hardened themselves therein. When God's Son, whose coming had been foretold throughout the centuries, comes to fulfill and end the covenant, His relation to men again assumes the form of a covenant. The people of the first covenant crowns its disobedience by turning on the Messiah and killing Him; and the second covenant, which should have been sealed in faith and love, once again is sealed in sacrificial blood, now the blood of Jesus Christ.

For the Messiah accepts the destiny prepared for Him by the disobedient people of the first covenant and turns it into the sacrificial offering of the second, which binds the Father, Lord of the world, to His new people, now no longer a natural ethnic one, but a spiritual people, composed of all the races of the earth and united by faith.

Wherever a man opens his heart to the tidings of Christ and believes in Him, he becomes a member of that people, as St. Peter says in his first letter: "You, however, are a chosen race, a royal priesthood, a holy nation, a purchased people; that you may proclaim the perfections of Him who has called you out of the darkness into His marvelous light" (1 Pet. 2:9).

The new covenant, then, embraces a divine people which takes nothing from any earthly people and disturbs no national history, because it exists on an entirely different plane.

It is strange how completely the idea of the covenant has vanished from the Christian consciousness. We do mention it, but it seems to have lost its meaning for us. Rather, our Christian existence is determined by concepts of the new life, the new world, God's kingdom—all of which tend to attach themselves to corresponding concepts in the natural order and to masquerade as things self-understood. But the moment of unmasking always arrives. Then the seeming naturalness of the Christian conceptions falls, and we realize with a start that Christian being is no mere continuation of natural being, that the Christian order of existence is not simply a higher step in the order of nature and man, but descends to us from divine freedom and is meant to be caught up and held in human freedom. God summons man before Him. Upon hearing the divine command and question, man is meant to liberate himself from what is purely of this earth and to prove his loyalty to God—straight through the ties of the world. What then takes place is based not on nature, or the processes of history, or the unfolding of the mind and spirit, but on grace, summons, freedom, decision, all contained in the idea of the covenant.

We are Christians because of a covenant. This thought must complement the other, more familiar concept of rebirth and the new creation. Covenant and rebirth: individual dignity and responsibility, and the abundance of the new life. The two great concepts belong together, for they mutually sustain one another.

Holy Mass is the commemoration of God's new covenant with men. Awareness of this gives the celebration an added significance that is most salutary. To keep this thought in mind is to remind ourselves that Christ's sacrificial death opened for us the new heaven and the new earth; that there exists between Him and us a contract based not on nature or talent or religious capacity, but on grace and freedom; that it is binding from person to person, loyalty to loyalty. At every Mass we should reaffirm that contract and consciously take our stand in it.

33

The Mass and Christ's Return

"But I say to you, I will not drink henceforth of this fruit of the vine, until that day when I shall drink it new with you in the kingdom of my Father" (Matt. 26:29). Like the concept of the covenant, which we have just discussed, this word of Christ too has been strangely neglected. St. Luke places the passage after the offering of the last of the Passover cups and before the words that actually institute the Eucharist. Jesus seems to be gazing through and beyond the hour of the Last Supper to the coming of the Kingdom. He is referring to the future eternal fulfillment that lies somewhere behind the inevitable death toward which, in obedience to His Father's will, He now must stride. The passage tinges the whole memorial with a singular radiance which seems largely to have faded from the Christian consciousness.

It might be objected that this word was perhaps important to Jesus personally, but not for His eucharistic memorial; that before His death, the Lord's vision, grave and knowing, reached across the future to the end of all things; that this thought was part of the subjective experience of the hour, but it has nothing to do with the sacred act which henceforth is to stand at the core of Christian life.

But what St. Paul writes of the establishment of the Eucharist overturns all such theories:

> For I myself have received from the Lord (what I also delivered to you), that the Lord Jesus, on the night in which He was betrayed, took bread, and giving thanks broke, and said, "This is my body which shall be given up for you; do this in remembrance of me." In like manner also the cup, after He had supped, saying, "This cup is the new covenant in my blood; do this as often as you drink it, in remembrance of me." For as often as you shall eat this bread and drink this cup, you proclaim the death of the Lord until He comes. (1 Cor. 11:23-26)

Can anyone still speak seriously of a mere expression of Jesus' passing mood? Specifically St. Paul connects the last things with the celebration of the Lord's memorial, and we must not forget that the Apostle's letters are at least as early as, some of them earlier than, the Gospels, and that they voice the powerful religious consciousness of the first congregations.

From all this it is apparent that when the Lord instituted the Eucharist things appeared before His inner vision more or less as follows: He knew that on the next day He would die. He knew, furthermore, that one day He would return; although "of that day and hour no one knows, not even the angels of heaven, but the Father only" (Matt. 24:36). For the period between these two events He was establishing the memorial of His redemptory death. This was to be the strength and comfort of the oppressed (indeed, of all who looked forward to His coming), and a constant reminder of His glorious promise. Compared with that fulfillment, passing time with all its self-importance is really only marking time before the essential. Holy Mass, then, is distinctly eschatological, and we should be much more concerned about our forgetfulness of the fact.

But what is this eschatology that we meet so frequently in the newer literature? It is that which pertains to the last things, and it exists in a natural form in our consciousness of the fundamental uncertainty of existence. By this we do not mean any superficial uncertainty connected with our personal existence or with general existence, although this is of course part of it, but the underlying uncertainty of all existence.

There are some individuals who know nothing of this. In fact, it has been ignored by all in certain periods. For them the world is an unshakable reality—the reality, essential and self-understood. Everything in it is regulated by a definite order of things; everything has its obvious causes and sure results, its clear, universally recognized value. But at certain periods all this changes. Usage seems to lose its validity. The whole structure of human society is shaken.

Then accepted standards of work and propriety, the canons of taste and the rules of behavior grow uncertain. It is no longer possible to plan the future, for everything has become fluent. A feeling of universal danger creeps into man's consciousness and establishes itself there, resulting in forms of experience peculiar to persons of a certain sensibility. What seems self-understood to those firmly implanted in action and property appears to these singularly perceptive natures as thoroughly questionable. For them the existing order of things, indeed of life itself, seems but loosely, precariously balanced across the chaos of existence and its uncontrollable forces. All rules seem temporary and threaten to give way at any moment. Things themselves appear now shadowy, now ominous.

It is easy to reply that such feelings are typical of the emotional crises that accompany historical turning points and periods of personal turmoil; or that they are the reactions of an unsound, if not abnormal nature. This is possible; but it is also possible that they express something completely normal: the truth. The sense of the uncertainty of existence is just as well founded as that of its opposite — that of the certainty of existence. Only the two forms of experience together contain the whole truth. These vague sensations so difficult to express and still more difficult to interpret receive their clear significance from revelation, which warns us that all is certainly not well with the world; that on the contrary, human nature is profoundly disordered; that its seeming health and stability are questionable precisely because they conceal that disorder.

It revealed itself openly when the Creator and Lord of the world "came unto His own; and His own received Him not" (John 1:11). Instead, they did everything possible to destroy Him. True, His death did redeem the world; within His love a new, real protection and an eternally stable order did come into being; nevertheless, the stain of the world's turning on its God and crushing Him remains.

He whom the world attempted to destroy will come again, to end it and to judge it. No one knows when, but come He will. Although we cannot imagine such a thing, the world will perish, and not by its own folly or from any natural cause. Christ will put an end to it in the age and hour "which the Father has fixed by His own authority" (Acts 1:7). Thus Christian existence must face the constant possibility of a sudden end, irrespective of life's apparent security, order, and promise. Now we begin to see what those sensations of uncertainty really mean: threat from the periphery of time, from Christ, who will come "to judge the living and the dead," as we say in the Credo. The memorial of His suffering and redemption, which He placed at the heart of our present existence, is oriented toward that Coming. It reminds us how things really stand with us.

34

Expecting the Lord

Early Christianity was acutely conscious of the imminence of Christ's coming. We see this in references to it in the Acts and feel it in the letters of St. Paul. Even the book of Revelation, written at the turn of the century, ends with the words of expectation: "And the Spirit and the bride say, 'Come!' And let him who hears say, 'Come!'... He who testifies to these things says, 'It is true, I come quickly!' 'Amen! Come, Lord Jesus!'" (Rev. 22:17-21). In other very early Christian writings as well, there is a great sense of expectancy. The Lord will return — and soon.

Then gradually the feeling that His coming is imminent disappears, and the faithful settle down for a longer period. While the persecutions lasted (in other words, well into the fourth century), however, existence was so precarious that the sense of the unreality of earthly things was kept very much alive. Then Christianity became the official state religion, the solid, accepted form of life, and the sense of general insecurity vanished. As we have seen, it reappears in periods of historical upset and in certain particular natures, but it no longer determines the Christian bearing as such.

Thus Christian existence has lost its eschatological quality, very much to its detriment, because with that loss the sense of belonging to the world becomes more or less self-understood. Christianity's intrinsic watchfulness and readiness are gone. It forgets that the words "Watch and pray!" (Matt. 26:41; Mark 14:38) are meant not only morally, as a vital sense of responsibility to the divine will, but also essentially, as a manner of being. The Christian is never meant to settle down in the world or become one with nature, or with business or art.

Essentially a soldier, the Christian is always on the lookout. He has sharper ears and hears an undertone that others miss; his eyes see things in a particularly candid light, and he senses something to which others are insensible, the streaming of a vital current through all things. He is never submerged in life, but keeps his head and shoulders clear of it and his eyes free to look upward. Consequently he has a deeper sense of responsibility than others. When this awareness and watchfulness disappear, Christian life loses its edge; it becomes dull and ponderous.

Then, too, Holy Mass loses one of the marks which the Lord Himself impressed upon it, a mark which the early Christians were aware of. It becomes a firmly established custom, the accepted, Christ-given form in which to praise, give thanks, seek help, practice atonement and generally determine religious existence. Then the Mass becomes that which is celebrated in every church every day at a certain time, and above all on Sunday. This is of course correct, as far as it goes — certainly not very far. Something essential is lacking.

Perhaps it will find its way back into our lives and the Mass. The different aspects of God's word have different seasons. At times the one will fade, retreat into the background, even vanish from the Christian consciousness. It is still there in Scripture and continues to be read in the Liturgy, but the words are no longer heard. Then the direction of existence shifts, and the same words seem to ring out, suddenly eloquent. Today history is undergoing such a change. It is breaking out of its former impregnability into a period of revolutionary destruction and reconstruction. The old sense of stability and permanence is no longer strong enough to provide the mystery of existence with the answers. We have again become profoundly conscious of life's transitoriness and questionableness. Thus even the natural situation helps us to understand St. Paul's, "For the world as we see it is passing away" (1 Cor. 7:31). Anything can happen. We begin to be aware of the magnitude of divine possibility, begin to sense the reality of Christ's coming, that pressing toward us from the edge of time, "for I say to you that I will not drink of the fruit of the vine, until the kingdom of God comes" (Luke 22:18).

Jesus' words just before the institution of the Eucharist are not there by chance. The celebration of the Lord's memorial binds the present moment not only to eternity — a thought we readily understand — but also to the future; a future, however, that lies not in time, but that approaches it from beyond and that will ultimately abolish time. Christ's promise teaches us to reevaluate the present, the better to persevere in it.

How well we understand the mood that must have prevailed in the early Christian congregations. Those people knew: everything around us is uncertain, alien, edged with danger. No one knows what tomorrow will bring. Now, however, we are here, celebrating the memorial of our Lord. He knows about us, and we know about Him. He is the One who dictates the apocalyptical letters: "I know thy works ... and thy patience ... and thy tribulation and thy poverty.... I know where thou dwellest" (Rev. 2:2, 9, 13). The Lord "knows everything." This knowledge is our refuge. Now, at the moment of sacred commemoration, He will come to us, will be with us, will fortify us. Whatever tomorrow may bring, it will be of His sending.

The celebration of the Mass should always be tinged by the feeling: the world "is passing away" (1 Cor. 7:31). A temporal thing from the start, it spins before God's eternity for as long as He permits it to do so. But its essential temporality is not all; it is seconded by an acquired temporality or mortality, the extreme disorder brought about by its disobedience and injustice. Once summoned before God's judgment, the world will be unable to stand. When that summons is to come, we do not know; hence the admonition to watch and pray so as not to be found "sleeping" (Mark 14:40; Matt. 26:43). All that is certain is that it will come soon, the word signifying no simple measure of time (tomorrow rather than a year, for instance, or thirty years rather than thousands) but an essential soon, applicable to all time, no matter how long it lasts. It is the sacred soon that comes to us from the quiet waiting of Christ, pressing terrible and blissful from the limits of time upon every hour, and belonging somehow in our own consciousness if our faith is to be complete.

All this seems strange to us. We must be honest and not pretend to something we do not really feel. Here is a task for our Christian self-education. We must try to feel our way into these thoughts; must gradually make this expectancy our own. Then Holy Mass will receive an entirely new significance. We will realize how essential it is for us, and it will become an hour of profoundest tranquillity and assurance. Throughout the noise and tension of the day, thought of the Mass will sustain us. The mind will reach out to it like a hand stretched out — each time to receive new strength.

Romano Guardini
(1885-1968)

Although he was born in Verona, Italy, Romano Guardini grew up in Mainz, Germany, where his father was serving as Italian consul. Since his education and formation were German, he decided to remain in Germany as an adult.

After studying chemistry and economics as a youth, Guardini turned to theology and was ordained to the priesthood in 1910. From 1923 to 1939 (when he was expelled by the Nazis), Father Guardini occupied a chair especially created for him at the University of Berlin as "professor for philosophy of religion and Catholic Weltanschauung." After the war, similar positions were created for him — first at the University of Tübingen and then at the University of Munich (1948-1963).

Father Guardini's extremely popular courses in these universities won him a reputation as one of the most remarkable and successful Catholic educators in Germany. As a teacher, a writer, and a speaker, he was notable for being able to detect and nurture those elements of spirituality that nourish all that is best in the life of Catholics.

After the war, Father Guardini's influence grew to be enormous, not only through his university positions, but also through the inspiration and guidance he gave to the post-war German Catholic Youth Movement, which enlivened the faith of countless young people.

Father Guardini's writings include works on meditation, education, literature, art, philosophy, and theology. Among his dozens of books, perhaps the most famous is *The Lord*, which has been continuously in print in many languages since its first publication in 1937. Even today, countless readers continue to be transformed by these books, which combine a profound thirst for God with great depth of thought and a delightful perfection of expression. The works of Father Guardini are indispensable reading for anyone who wants to remain true to the Faith and to grow holy in our age of skepticism and corrosive doubt.

Sophia Institute

Sophia Institute is a nonprofit institution that seeks to nurture the spiritual, moral, and cultural life of souls and to spread the Gospel of Christ in conformity with the authentic teachings of the Roman Catholic Church.

Sophia Institute Press fulfills this mission by offering translations, reprints, and new publications that afford readers a rich source of the enduring wisdom of mankind.

Sophia Institute also operates two popular online Catholic resources: CrisisMagazine.com and CatholicExchange.com.

Crisis Magazine provides insightful cultural analysis that arms readers with the arguments necessary for navigating the ideological and theological minefields of the day. *Catholic Exchange* provides world news from a Catholic perspective as well as daily devotionals and articles that will help you to grow in holiness and live a life consistent with the teachings of the Church.

In 2013, Sophia Institute launched Sophia Institute for Teachers to renew and rebuild Catholic culture through service to Catholic education. With the goal of nurturing the spiritual, moral, and cultural life of souls, and an abiding respect for the role and work of teachers, we strive to provide materials and programs that are at once enlightening to the mind and ennobling to the heart; faithful and complete, as well as useful and practical.

Sophia Institute gratefully recognizes the Solidarity Association for preserving and encouraging the growth of our apostolate over the course of many years. Without their generous and timely support, this book would not be in your hands.

www.SophiaInstitute.com
www.CatholicExchange.com
www.CrisisMagazine.com
www.SophiaInstituteforTeachers.org

Sophia Institute Press® is a registered trademark of Sophia Institute.
Sophia Institute is a tax-exempt institution as defined by the
Internal Revenue Code, Section 501(c)(3). Tax I.D. 22-2548708.